For John Eisner

Rajiv Joseph

DESCRIBE THE NIGHT

OBERON BOOKS
LONDON

WWW.OBERONBOOKS.COM

First published in 2017 by Oberon Books Ltd
521 Caledonian Road, London N7 9RH
Tel: +44 (0) 20 7607 3637 / Fax: +44 (0) 20 7607 3629
e-mail: info@oberonbooks.com
www.oberonbooks.com

A catalogue record for this book is available from the British Library.

PB ISBN: 9781786823762
E ISBN: 9781786823779

Cover image by SWD

Visit www.oberonbooks.com to read more about all our books and to buy them. You
will also find features, author interviews and news of any author events, and you can
sign up for e-newsletters so that you're always first to hear about our new releases.

Describe the Night was first presented in 2014 in a student production at New York University's Graduate Acting Program, Mark Wing-Davey, Chair. It was developed at TheatreWorks, Palo Alto, CA as part of their New Works Festival.

The world premiere of *Describe the Night* was commissioned and produced by the Alley Theatre in Houston, TX in 2017.

The cast was as follows:
Jason Babinsky as VOVA
Jeffrey Bean as ISAAC
Elizabeth Bunch as MARIYA
Melissa Pritchett as URZULA
Liv Rooth as YEVGENIA
Stephen Stocking as FELIKS
Todd Waite as NIKOLAI

Directed by Giovanna Sardelli; Scenic Design by Tim Mackabee; Costume Design by Amy Clark; Lighting Design by Lap Chi Chu; Original Composition and Sound Design by Daniel Kluger; Stage Managed by Lori Lundquist.

Artistic Director – Gregory Boyd
Managing Director – Dean R. Gladden

The New York premiere of *Describe the Night* opened at Atlantic Theater Company on December 5, 2017.

The cast was as follows:
Tina Benko as YEVGENIA
Nadia Bowers as MARIYA, MRS. PETROVNA
Danny Burstein as ISAAC
Zach Grenier as NIKOLAI
Rebecca Naomi Jones as URZULA
Max Gordon Moore as VOVA
Stephen Stocking as FELIKS

Directed by Giovanna Sardelli; Scenic Design by Tim Mackabee; Costume Design by Amy Clark; Lighting Design by Lap Chi Chu; Original Compositions and Sound Design by Daniel Kluger; Wig Design by Leah Loukas; Fight Choreography by J. David Brimmer; Stage Managed by Lori Lundquist; Casting by Telsey + Co. Will Cantler, CSA, Adam Caldwell, CSA, Karyn Casl, CSA

Artistic Director – Neil Pepe
Managing Director – Jeffory Lawson

The London premiere of *Describe the Night* opened at Hampstead Theatre on April 30, 2018.

The cast was as follows:
David Birrell as NIKOLAI
Ben Caplan as ISAAC
Siena Kelly as URZULA
Wendy Kweh as MARIYA, MRS. PETROVNA
Joel MacCormack as FELIKS
Rebecca O'Mara as YEVGENIA
Steve John Shepherd as VOVA

Director – Lisa Spirling
Designer – Polly Sullivan
Lighting Designer – Johanna Town
Composer and Sound Designer – Richard Hammarton
Movement Director – Chi-San Howard
Casting – Annelie Powell CDG

Characters

ISAAC*

Russian, Jewish. He is the writer Isaac Babel.

In 1920 he is twenty-five years old. A quiet, shy young man with dreams of being a successful writer, but traumatized from the Polish-Russo war, where he is a wire-service journalist – a job he took in order to experience something in life he could write about.

In 1937-40 he is a successful writer of fiction and films. He has robust appetites, and is far more self-assured, he is not intimidated by anyone. He craves danger.

NIKOLAI*

Russian. Last name: Yezhov. A Captain in the Russian Red Cavalry in 1920, when he is thirty years old. He is enormously self-assured, an accomplished military man. A violent man.

In 1937-40, he is the Head of Stalin's Secret Police which will become the KGB.

In 1989, when he is ninety-four, he is a living relic of Russian history, and knows it. He enjoys tormenting young KGB agents.

YEVGENIA*

Russian, the wife of Nikolai Yezhov. In 1940, she is thirty-six. Bright, beautiful, drawn to astrology and supernatural topics. Unhappy in her marriage, but would never say so.

In 1989 she is eighty-six years old. Mischievous, with a humor that is rooted in pain and tragedy.

VOVA*

Russian, a KGB agent stationed in Dresden, East Germany,
in 1989, at which time he is thirty-five years old.

In 2010, he is a politician of enormous stature.
Deeply self-assured, yet terrified of the world.

URZULA

Polish, and in 1989, an immigrant, living in Dresden.
The grand-daughter of Yevgenia.

FELIKS

Polish. Thin, covered with tattoos, a dreary disposition.
An orphan. At twenty-one, in 2010, he feels middle-aged.

MARIYA

Russian, thirties, a journalist for a state-run newspaper in 2010.
Moscow born and bred. Strong and steady.

MRS. PETROVNA

Russian, seventies, the owner of a laundromat.
Played by actress who plays Mariya.

Note: Actors should not speak in any dialect.

What time in human history is comparable to this? It's nearly impossible to locate plausible occasions for hope. Foulness, corruption, meanness of spirit carry the day. I think a lot about 1939, of the time the Russian writer Victor Serge called "the midnight of the century," when women and men of good conscience, having witnessed the horrors of World War I, watched helplessly, overwhelmed by despair, as fascism and war made their inexorable approaches; as Leninism transformed into Stalinism; a time like this one, when, in Brecht's immortal phrase "there is injustice everywhere/ and no rebellion." ...

... Tragedy is the annihilation from whence new life springs, the Nothing out which Something is born. Devastation can be a necessary prelude to a new kind of beauty. Necessary but always bloody. In the preface to his verse drama, Cain, Byron tells us: "The world was destroyed many times before the creation of man." That makes a certain sort of sense to me, the history of revolution and modern evolutionary theory lend credence to Byron's breathtaking assertion, but how frightening! Are cataclysm and catastrophe the birth spasms of the future, is the mass grave some sort of cradle, does the future always arrive borne on a torrent of blood?

Tony Kushner, From *An Afterword* to *Homebody/Kabul*

The seed of the Coast of Utopia was an episode in the career of Vissarion Belinsky, a literary critic who worked in Moscow and St Petersburg in the 1830s and 1840s. In 1847 Belinsky was permitted to travel to Germany for his health. From Salzbrunn he went to Paris, where he found himself among new and old friends from home. They attempted to persuade Belinsky not to return to Russia, where he lived a precarious existence under the malign gaze of the Tsarist secret police, but to remain in Paris, where he would be able to live freely and above all to write freely.

But Belinsky was having none of it. He replied that in St Petersburg, under punitive censorship, the public looked to writers as their real leaders. The title of poet, novelist or critic really counted. In Paris, on the contrary, it was almost impossible to be heard in the general din. In Paris no writing mattered very much, and most writing didn't matter at all. So Belinsky went home. His name was on a list of people to be arrested, but consumption caught up with him first and he was dead within a year.

Tom Stoppard, From the introduction to *The Coast of Utopia*

No one lives his life.

Disguised since childhood,
haphazardly assembled
from voices and fears and little pleasures,
we come of age as masks.

Our true face never speaks.

Somewhere there must be storehouses
where all these lives are laid away
like suits of armor or old carriages
or clothes hanging limply on the walls.

Maybe all paths lead there,
to the repository of unlived things.

Rainer Maria Rilke, *Book of Hours*, II,ii

Chapter Headings

ACT I

1. Lies – 1920 – Polish Countryside (Isaac, Nikolai)

2. Car Rental – 2010 – Smolensk (Feliks, Mariya)

3. Fate – 1937 – Moscow (Isaac, Nikolai, Yevgenia)

4. Bureau 42 – 1989 – Moscow (Vova, Nikolai)

ACT II

1. Blood – 1989 – Dresden (Vova, Yevgenia, Urzula)

2. Asylum – 1940 – Moscow (Nikolai, Isaac)

3. Escape – 1940 – Moscow (Yevgenia, Isaac)

4. Glasnost – 1989 – Moscow (Vova, Nikolai)

ACT III

1. Freedom – 1989 – Dresden (Yevgenia, Vova)

2. More Lies – 1940 – Moscow (Isaac, Nikolai)

3. Silence – 2010 – Moscow (Mariya, Vova)

4. Laundry – 2010 – Moscow (Yevgenia, Feliks, Mrs. Petrovna)

Act I

The countryside, not far from the Russian border.

Night.

ISAAC, twenties, a member of the Russian Red Cavalry, sits on a rock or a stump, apart from the troops. He's seen a lot today. He tries to write in his journal.

ISAAC: Describe the night...

(He writes this; he thinks.)

A patchwork.
A sullen patchwork of...
A sullen patchwork of stars...

(He writes this, then scratches it out, and thinks again.)

Stupid...

(Makes himself write again.)

Describe the air.

(He thinks; can't describe it, tries something else.)

Describe the field...

(He looks at it.)

Brown.

(Doesn't like this.)

A... a cemetery of... of... weeds...

(Makes a disgusted face.)

(Breathes deeply.)

He writes something and then stares at what he wrote. It's a truth and it's not necessarily a happy one.

NIKOLAI, a brusque, imposing soldier enters. Sees ISAAC writing. NIKOLAI lights a cigarette. ISAAC senses him, and shuts his book, not wanting to speak to NIKOLAI or be noticed by him.

NIKOLAI: Writing.

ISAAC: What?

NIKOLAI: Writing, writing. This is you:

(He pantomimes furious writing.)

Writing.

ISAAC: It's what I do.

NIKOLAI: *Babel, I.* Correspondent. YugROSTA. Wire Service.

ISAAC: Yes, that's me, it's what I do.

NIKOLAI: *Babel, I.* "I" stands for?

ISAAC: Isaac.

NIKOLAI: What?

ISAAC: Isaac…

NIKOLAI: What?

ISAAC: Isaac.

NIKOLAI: *Isaac.* Isaac Babel.

(Introduces himself.)

Yezhov, N. "N" stands for: Nikolai.

ISAAC: Yes, I know, I know who you are.

NIKOLAI: What kind of accent is that?

ISAAC: I'm not sure. Odessa.

NIKOLAI: Jew?

ISAAC: What kind of accent is yours?

NIKOLAI: Standard Russian. Straight across the middle. Little to no affect. Man of the People.

What are you writing? A report for today? Wire services? *"Here is the war. Here is the war in writing. So you who are not here, at the war, can know what the war is like."*

(Beat; he expects ISAAC to respond, but ISAAC doesn't.)

So? Is that the wire report?

ISAAC: No. Just writing.

NIKOLAI: Just writing what?

ISAAC: In my journal.

NIKOLAI: A journal is for journalists.

ISAAC: No, my journal is my diary. Personal reflections on my daily life.

NIKOLAI: I don't understand you. Maybe the accent.

ISAAC: Okay.

NIKOLAI: Okay what?

ISAAC: Okay, you don't understand me.

NIKOLAI: Army journalist, correspondent from YugROSTA, you report on such events as the Red Cavalry does. You send reports across the wire. Such reports are based on observations, or, as you say, "personal reflections". You have a "journal" in which you write these. But your reports to YugROSTA: not personal reflection?

ISAAC: Not really, no.

NIKOLAI: Then they are lies!

ISAAC: I mean, I write facts.

NIKOLAI: Facts, then. Facts are not personal reflections?

ISAAC: My diary is just for me to write to myself.

NIKOLAI: I don't understand you. Maybe the accent.

ISAAC: Sometimes I write to myself to make sense of the day.

NIKOLAI: Point is, Correspondent Babel: The report for today. What of it?

ISAAC: Today?

NIKOLAI: Today's actions. What did you write today?

ISAAC realizes why NIKOLAI is here.

ISAAC: Today?

NIKOLAI: YOUR REPORT! HAVE YOU WRITTEN IT?

ISAAC: Not yet.

NIKOLAI: When?

ISAAC: Commander Yezhov, you can be assured – I won't.

NIKOLAI: You won't what?

ISAAC: *(Trying to spit this out.)* You are concerned that I will write about you. What you did today. That I will send it along the wire.

NIKOLAI: *(Flustered.)* Write what you will write, I don't care what you write, as long as you write facts! As long as everything is TRUE.

ISAAC: *(Sighs; in despair.)* I don't know what's true. I'm the worst person to determine what is true.

NIKOLAI: Don't be stupid. True is what happens. False is what does not happen.

(Beat.)

Writers.

I don't care what you write.

So a man was killed today in Zhitomir. This happens. I did it in front of everybody and everybody saw, and the man had an axe.

ISAAC: Of course.

NIKOLAI: The man had an axe.

ISAAC: I know.

NIKOLAI: And so the man was killed.

It doesn't matter if he was old. If he was very old.
Old people fight, too.
Old people die, too.
If you are old, and if you have an axe, and if you approach a soldier, a soldier like me... then you should expect...
You should know what to expect.

ISAAC: I agree with you. And anyhow it wasn't newsworthy.

NIKOLAI: It wasn't?

ISAAC: No. Wire services want basic, generalizations, with a touch of humanity.

NIKOLAI: I have humanity.

ISAAC: Of course you do.

NIKOLAI: But you don't write about me.

ISAAC: Not to date.

NIKOLAI: I'm saying, in the future, you could write about me. About my humanity.

ISAAC: Of course.

NIKOLAI: You're saying you will?

ISAAC: If something happens newsworthy, yes.

NIKOLAI: Right, well, you wouldn't just make something up. True is what happens. False is what does not happen.

Awkward beat between them. NIKOLAI tosses his cigarette, checks, finds he is out of cigarettes.

NIKOLAI: There are never enough cigarettes.

Beat.

ISAAC: Describe the night.

NIKOLAI: What?

ISAAC: The night. Describe it.

NIKOLAI: Which night?

ISAAC: This night. Right here. Now.

NIKOLAI: Why?

ISAAC: I just described it in my journal. I'm wondering how you would describe it. And if we both describe the same thing at the same time, will one of our descriptions be more true than the other?

NIKOLAI: What? No! Shut up.

(Beat; he decides to describe the night.)

Black.
Quiet.
Not so quiet,
Not so black.
I don't know, the night can't be described.
The night is for sleeping.
The night is for smoking when one can't sleep.

(He looks off in the distance.)

Low in the eastern sky, over there: Venus.

ISAAC: Where?

NIKOLAI: That glow, there. Venus is called a Morning Star, but it's not a star, it's a planet.

(Beat.)

How did you describe the night?

ISAAC hands him his book. NIKOLAI reads it.

NIKOLAI: Mine is more true than yours. This doesn't make any sense. Too many words.

NIKOLAI reads other pages of the book.

ISAAC: Don't read the rest… it's personal…

NIKOLAI walks away, engrossed in it. Getting angry.

NIKOLAI: WHAT THE HELL IS THIS!?

ISAAC: It's nothing! It's not supposed to be true! Give it back!

NIKOLAI: You said facts! These aren't facts!

ISAAC: That's not for the wire report, damnit, it's just my personal diary!

NIKOLAI: THIS ISN'T REAL!

ISAAC: Of course it isn't real! I told you that! Give it back!

NIKOLAI: The daughter didn't cry out like this! She didn't cry out like this when he was killed. She simply knelt beside him and cleaned his face. She didn't cry out.

(Beat.)

And you blame the Poles for this. When it was me who killed the old man, not the Poles.

DON'T LIE ABOUT ME!

ISAAC: Have you ever put your nose into the ass of a goat and just breathed in?

NIKOLAI: What? No!

ISAAC: If you do this, then you can read people's minds.

NIKOLAI: That's not… read their minds how?

ISAAC: The gaseous interiors of a goat inspire supernatural clarity.

NIKOLAI: *What?*

ISAAC: I love goat ass, I love reading minds.

NIKOLAI: *(Looks around, nervous.)* Where are these goats?

ISAAC: Ah, but I have such advanced powers of smell, I detect goat ass from miles away!

NIKOLAI: Really?

ISAAC: NO! None of these things are true! I've never smelled a goat ass, I can't read people's minds! Am I a liar? No, I'm not. *I tell stories.* Stay out of my diary.

A moment of shocked silence and then NIKOLAI laughs hysterically, truly impressed at ISAAC.

NIKOLAI: You made all that up? You just invented it!?

ISAAC shrugs. NIKOLAI is astounded, impressed.

NIKOLAI: No… no… whoa… Tell me another lie.

ISAAC: My father was a French spy.

NIKOLAI: Really?

ISAAC: No.

NIKOLAI erupts in laughter again.

NIKOLAI: Tell me another!

ISAAC: I only have seven toes.

NIKOLAI: Really?

ISAAC: No.

NIKOLAI: How do you DO that!?

ISAAC: I stole some wine from the Zhitomir cathedral, would you like to share it with me?

NIKOLAI: *(Laughing.)* Too much! Too much!

ISAAC takes a small bottle from his coat.

ISAAC: No, I'm serious, I stole some wine. Look: Wine. Unconsecrated. Not yet the blood of Christ, but still wine.

NIKOLAI smiles.

NIKOLAI: I like you!

He sits next to ISAAC. They share sips of wine.

Wondrous lies!

ISAAC: Thank you.

NIKOLAI: (Tasting wine; wincing.)

Ugh... Polish wine.

ISAAC: It's no wonder... Here in Poland, wine is made from squeezing bread, not grapes.

NIKOLAI: Really?

ISAAC: No.

NIKOLAI: *(Smiles.)* You are different, Isaac Babel. You are different.

ISAAC: Writers are different than soldiers.

NIKOLAI: But here we sit, together, under the same Polish sky, drinking Polish wine, suffering through Poland.

(Beat; sadly.) The food is different here.

ISAAC: In these parts of rural Poland, they have a leech soup...

NIKOLAI: That is disgusting.

ISAAC: A national delicacy. Lukewarm broth with living leeches swimming within. Once served, you prick your finger with a needle, and dip your bleeding fingertips into the soup. The leeches immediately begin to feed upon your blood, and they engorge themselves. And then you eat the soup, *and* the engorged leeches.

NIKOLAI: But why?

ISAAC: They say it cures forgetfulness.

NIKOLAI: But *how?!*

ISAAC smiles.

NIKOLAI: No… a lie? Another *Lie?*

(He smiles, puts his arm around ISAAC.)

I can't believe how good at lying you are.

Beat.

ISAAC: Tell me a lie.

NIKOLAI: How?

ISAAC: Make something up.

NIKOLAI: I can't.

ISAAC: Everyone can.

NIKOLAI: I don't know how.

ISAAC: Just prepare to say something true, and then say the opposite.

NIKOLAI looks like he's thinking, prepares to say something, then can't.

NIKOLAI: I can't. Lies are lies are lies.

I can't.

Beat. They drink.

NIKOLAI: The old man was actually an old woman.

And she…
She had twenty-two children.
No, I don't like that.
The old man was an old man and he had an axe.
Maybe it wasn't an axe.

My lie is: The old man didn't have an axe, he had a shovel.
And he was going to dig a grave.

For his son.

And he wasn't angry or attacking, but merely weeping.
And I didn't like the sight of him weeping and dressed in stupid rags and the idea of digging a grave for his son was disgusting to me so I cut his throat and the world is happier for it.

Is that a lie?

ISAAC: Is that a lie?

NIKOLAI: I'm asking you.

ISAAC: Only you can say.

NIKOLAI is pained, but takes the pain and puts it away and never feels it again.

NIKOLAI: It is a lie. A man attacked me with an axe and so I killed him.

You are better at lying than me.

Beat. They drink.

ISAAC: Is that really Venus?

NIKOLAI: Particularly visible this month, at this hour.

ISAAC: How do you know about planets?

NIKOLAI: My wife studies these sorts of things. You would like her. She thinks she can predict the future.

ISAAC: Is she ever right?

NIKOLAI: Nah. All she predicts is war. What sort of prediction is that?

ISAAC: And yet, here we are. At war.

NIKOLAI: I say to her, *well, darling, if all you do is predict the same thing over and over, then it's not really a prediction.*

War.

There will be *war*.

What kind of prophecy is that?

Wars should be done by now.

ISAAC: But they're not.

NIKOLAI: No. They're not.

And anyhow we aren't at war. Not at this moment.

ISAAC: We aren't?

NIKOLAI: No, look. Look:

The sky is like a chandelier in Moscow.

And we are like men having tea.

And the crickets are some violins, and the horses breathing over there, are the quiet, soft murmuring of pretty women in the tea house.

(Beat.)

Maybe one of them is about to sing.

Terrible industrial sounds fill the space. The sounds of metal scraping, tearing, of engines and bulldozers.

Lights up on a dim and rundown, generic car rental office in Smolensk, Russia.

A young man stands at his window, blinds drawn, nervously peeking out through the slats.

This is FELIKS, twenty-one. He is thin, with closely cropped hair. Tattoos line his arms. He wears a tank top, old jeans.

He leaves the window and pours what is probably another glass of vodka. He sits and drinks it.

The sounds in the distance continue at various intervals. It's daylight, but there is a deep fog outside. You can barely see a few feet in front of you.

Every so often, lights of traffic glow through the windows. Sometimes sirens. Sounds of machinery...

Suddenly, the front door rattles, as if someone trying to get in. FELIKS stands up in fright and stares at it. An urgent knock.

More knocks at the door.

A woman's voice...

FELIKS: Who is it.

MARIYA (O.S.): Hello, are you open? Hello?!

FELIKS: Who is it?!

MARIYA (O.S.): I want to rent a car.

FELIKS: We're closed.

> *A beat. FELIKS waits, hoping she goes away... But more knocking, more insistent.*

FELIKS: *(Louder.)* We're *closed!*

MARIYA (O.S.): *(With a hint of despair.)* Please... can you help me?

FELIKS does not want to open the door. But he goes to it. He unlocks two locks and cautiously opens the door part of the way. MARIYA, thirties.

FELIKS: We're closed!

MARIYA gets in.

FELIKS: No fuckin' way, Lady!

MARIYA: I need to rent a car.

FELIKS: *(With aggression.)* We're closed, how many times I gotta tell you!

MARIYA: Look, it's freezing out there. You can help me out, right? I can tell you're a good guy.

FELIKS: I ain't a charity!

MARIYA: I just need to –

FELIKS: *I don't need people pounding on my door today!*

MARIYA: No, I wanted –

FELIKS: You wanted what? Huh? You wanted what? We are CLOSED and so *I* want you out of here NOW before I –

MARIYA: NO! NO! YOU DON'T YELL AT ME! I'VE HAD A REAL FUCKING BAD DAY AND I DON'T CARE IF YOU'RE CLOSED I NEED TO RENT A FUCKING CAR, SO LET ME DO THAT AND I WILL LEAVE YOU ALONE!

As if both startled by their respective ferocity, they just stand there in awkward silence...

FELIKS: I only have mid-size sedans.

MARIYA: Good yeah. That's fine.

Insane sounds rattle and erupt from outside. Lights flash through the windows. It feels like the end of the world.

FELIKS goes to the other side of the counter. He takes a clipboard.

FELIKS: How long?

MARIYA: How long for what?

FELIKS: *(Irritated.) How long you wanna rent the car for?*

MARIYA: Okay! I got it! One day. Just, only… one day.

FELIKS: License…

MARIYA: What?

FELIKS: Driver's license… do you have one? Necessary. And credit card.

She gives him both. Then, the monstrous sound of a machine outside the window, and lights flood through the blinds. They both just stand there, watching the glow.

FELIKS: Fill this out. Please write legibly. I have a hard time reading messy handwriting.

MARIYA: Okay, well that's good, because I have very legible handwriting.

FELIKS: I'm not making a joke.

MARIYA: Okay.

She begins to fill out the form.

MARIYA: Can I return the car in Moscow?

FELIKS: That requires an additional form.

MARIYA: I don't care about forms!

FELIKS: And you gotta rent it for a full week, with full insurance. And that's non-negotiable, it's non-negotiable!

MARIYA: Why are you yelling at me?!

FELIKS: I'm telling you the rules!

MARIYA: You don't need to yell.

FELIKS: I didn't need to let you in here either!

MARIYA: And I'm thankful, okay? So thank you.

(Beat.)

What's your accent? Are you Polish?

FELIKS: No.

MARIYA: You're not?

FELIKS: No.

MARIYA: Where're you from?

FELIKS: Nowhere. Warsaw. Poland. Yeah, okay, I'm Polish. *Why?* You got a problem with that?

MARIYA: Do you *know* who was on that airplane?

FELIKS: I dunno. People.

MARIYA: The President of *Poland* was on that airplane. The President and the First Lady and the Vice President and… and the entire government of Poland was on that airplane and now… they're…

FELIKS: That's not true.

MARIYA: It is.

FELIKS: No it's not! That's a lie. It was just a normal plane with normal people!

MARIYA: Did you see it crash?

FELIKS: What? *No.*

I didn't see it.

I didn't see it, it was in the corner of my line of sight, I was outside. I was looking away.

MARIYA: You saw it?

FELIKS: That's not what I said! I heard it and I saw an explosion.

MARIYA: You saw it explode…

FELIKS: I guess when a plane crashes it explodes! There was fog! They came in too close. They hit the tops of the trees in the woods and there was nothing left to do.

MARIYA: So you saw it crash.

FELIKS: *No.* What I just said, that's what I *inferred.*

(Beat; eyes her warily again.)

The police cut the whole area off. This whole area...
nobody can come in here.
Why are you here?
Who are you?

MARIYA: I came with a crew of reporters.

FELIKS: *(A whole new irritation.)* You're a *reporter?*

MARIYA: Yes...

FELIKS: You didn't tell me that! You should say something like that, you should say it outright!

MARIYA: I'm not here writing about... *that!*
I only came down here to do a stupid human interest story on the President and the first lady of Poland, who are now *dead...* right over there in the woods. Along with everyone else... they're all gone...

FELIKS goes to the window and peers through it. Looking around, perhaps to see if she was followed.

FELIKS: That's not what happened.

MARIYA: Yes it is.

FELIKS: You're not supposed to be here... They're looking for you, aren't they?

MARIYA: No, I ...

FELIKS: You come barging in here! Your pants are dirty!
You're trying to escape, and now I'm helping you...

MARIYA: They don't know I'm here! There were like ten of us in the press room, and I went out to smoke and the plane crashed, and then I... I watched them lead the reporters into a police van... everyone was arrested just because they were *there!* And my one friend in the bunch, this guy Yuri, who's big, you know, he's like a big guy, starts asking questions and they...

They clubbed him in the head and he...

He just went down.

And so I've spent the last six hours hiding in a dumpster.

FELIKS: In a what?

MARIYA: A big metal dumpster for trash! You know what I'm talking about! A dumpster! So I'm not exactly a reporter at this precise moment, I'm just a very scared person who wants to get the hell out of Smolensk!

FELIKS: What do you think you're going to do? Rent a car and then drive out down the road? There's police at every turn-off. You'll get stopped and picked up as soon as you leave.

This only just occurred to MARIYA. She has to sit down.

MARIYA: Fuck.

(To herself; with despair.)

What am I going to do?

(More to FELIKS.)

What am going to do?

He ignores her; he goes back to peering out the window.

MARIYA: Hey. What's your name?

FELIKS: I'm not telling you my *name.*

MARIYA: Fine. I'm just being friendly.

FELIKS: Well don't be.

MARIYA: I'm Mariya. Mariya Tokareva.

FELIKS: Great. So great. So great to meet you.

MARIYA: Look, can I stay here?

FELIKS: What?

MARIYA: You're right, I can't rent a car and drive down the street. I don't know what I was thinking, I've been… I've been…

(Takes a deep nervous breath; trying to keep it together.)

I've had a rough day, okay?

FELIKS: You can't *stay* here.

MARIYA: Not forever! Just until… *all that…* is over.

FELIKS: No, you can't stay here! Police have already been by here once, and they said they're coming back and so –

MARIYA: The police have been here?

FELIKS: What do you think? Of course they came here. And I didn't know why… They're lookin' around so much, I think maybe they wanted to rent a car. And they're giving it to me, asking questions, and it was off, something was wrong, they were going to kill me I thought…
And then one of them gets a call, and they're out of here. But said they'd be back, so now I'm sitting around waiting for *that* pleasant experience to continue. And so *No*, Mariya Tokareva, you can't *stay here*. The last thing I need is for police to come back here and find I'm harboring a fugitive reporter.

(Beat.)

I don't like police, and I don't like soldiers, and I don't like people who like police and soldiers, and I don't like people in general.

Another awful sound outside, metal, machinery… followed by a very muted, haunting sound that maybe, through the wind and fog and smoke, might be the sound of men laughing. But it could just as well be the wind, or birds.

FELIKS: You hear that…? I keep thinking I hear… like people laughing…

MARIYA: I hear it too. The same sound…

They look at each other and for the first, tenuous time, experience a shard of a connection.

FELIKS: Listen, there's an old access road, from before they renovated the airport, it's mostly covered over by weeds now, but it leads out of here and through an abandoned factory lot. There's a gate chained shut, but the chain is busted and if you slightly move the car into it, it'll pop. And then you have to hug this dirt road next to this swamp… it's like pure sewage, smells like death, and if the car falls in it would probably disintegrate, but that's a way out. That's a way you could drive if you wanted to get out. There won't be any police along that way, I guarantee you.

He goes behind the desk and finds a pair of keys.

FELIKS: I have an old truck out back, it's not even on my registry. You could take it.
Take it. Just get out before they come back.

As he hands the keys to her there's an explosion outside that makes them jump…

Then the lights go dead. Emergency lights come one. Then there are gunshots heard, men yelling, the screech of something ungodly… MARIYA and FELIKS are both so scared, she sits on the floor in a ball, and he scoots across the room and leans against his desk, both like frightened children.

The sounds that follow make no sense. Then it's silent again.

Both MARIYA and FELIKS sit across from each other, both afraid to move or speak.

FELIKS: *(Quietly.)* Mariya…

MARIYA: Are you okay?

FELIKS: No.

MARIYA: Me neither.

She scoots so she is nearer to him.

FELIKS: Don't move.

MARIYA: *(Whispers; says this more to God than anyone else.)*

What's happening out there?

FELIKS: Don't move!

MARIYA: Are they out there? Are they coming?

FELIKS: Yeah!

Long beat.

FELIKS: I did something bad. I did something… that I shouldn't have done…

(Beat.)

I went out there. I went into the woods.

MARIYA: You did? You went out there after the –

FELIKS: – Everything smelled of gasoline. I can't get the smell out of my nose, fuel. Gasoline. And there were airplane seats, chunked into the ground like tombstones. Just partial bodies in each one.
But there was a woman.
She was older, she was still alive. She sees me and she smiled at me.
She had a piece of metal coming out of her neck. But she was holding a book… she had a book in her hands and she handed it to me.

MARIYA: What was it?

FELIKS: A diary. A really old diary… I mean look at this…

He pulls out an old diary from under the desk. It is ISAAC Babel's diary from 1920.

FELIKS: It's from like 1920... I can't read most of it... it's very messy handwriting.

He hands it to her... But it's too dark for her to really look at it.

FELIKS: She handed it to me and I took it and she said, "thank you my son."

(Beat.)

Why would she say that to me?
Why's someone got to say something like that, and really formal too, as if she meant it, not like it was some nickname. People should think more when they have dying words especially if they utter them to strangers. I grew up in an *orphanage*, and this woman doesn't know that, but then she says something crazy like call me her son and then dies!?
What kind of messed up shit is that?

MARIYA: People see things when they die.

FELIKS: That's fine, they don't need to talk about it while they do.

Outside, the distant howling of a pterodactyl. Or something. MARIYA and FELIKS flinch in fear.

MARIYA: You grew up in an orphanage?

FELIKS: The Warsaw state commorancy for boys. Yeah.
It wasn't so bad.

(Beat.)

We used to play a game, "whose mother is worst?".
Sit around thinking up the worst people for our mothers.
It was the only way we could think about them. Ugly, whore witches who shit outside and then eat their shit.

MARIYA: Okay...

FELIKS: Look, we never imagined they were nice or sitting in a seat, dying, smiling, calling us "son".

Long beat.

MARIYA: She probably wasn't so nice.

FELIKS: Who?

MARIYA: That bitch in the seat. She was probably drank her own piss.

FELIKS: *(Manages a chuckle.)* Yeah...

MARIYA: She probably chewed her toenails off and ate them.

FELIKS: Yeah, she tortured animals.

MARIYA: With a fork she did.

FELIKS: Yeah. With a fork.

They quietly laugh, not hard, but just enough to relax microscopically. Gallows humor.

FELIKS: My name... My name is Feliks.

MARIYA: *Feliks*. That's a good name.

(Beat.)

What's happening out there?
Everywhere?

FELIKS: Bad stuff.

MARIYA: I'm sitting in that dumpster today, thinking... I was thinking I was going to die today. And I couldn't stop thinking about my landlady. This old lady... She runs a laundry and I live above it... She gives me a rate if I help her fold. She's mean and sour and she never smiles or laughs. And if I disappeared, the only person in the entire world who would notice would be her. Old Mrs. Petrovna.

FELIKS: *Mrs. Petrovna*. I can picture her.

MARIYA: Talk about terrible breath.

FELIKS: She probably steals one sock from every load of laundry she does.

MARIYA: That's not the half of it. I bet she's like former KGB or something.

FELIKS: She probably pulled people's fingernails out once upon a time.

MARIYA: No regrets either.

FELIKS: What a bitch.

MARIYA: She probably works for Putin. She probably crashed that plane herself.

Awkward beat.

FELIKS: That's not funny.

MARIYA: I'm just kidding.

FELIKS: Don't kid about that.

MARIYA: It's a joke.

FELIKS: Doesn't matter, don't joke about that.

MARIYA: Okay…

FELIKS: There was a fog and they hit the trees! Wasn't nothing on purpose!
People talk about everything like it's a big spy novel. Life isn't like that.

MARIYA: I know, I agree.

FELIKS: You "agree" but you're a media person, and so you you you love to make up stories that are more interesting than what the truth is and what the truth is that sometimes planes crash.

MARIYA: Clearly. Especially planes carrying the entire government of Poland.

FELIKS: Go ahead, write your news story about it, that's what they pay you for. But don't expect me to be any part of it.

MARIYA: I'm not writing anything about it, I'm not that kind of journalist. I write stupid puff pieces about nothing. I don't care about the world or important things anyway, so just relax.

They sit in silence for a moment. Then the lights come back on, normal. It's weird for both FELIKS and MARIYA, now having been sitting together, so close. They still don't move.

After a moment, FELIKS crawls over to the keys of the truck, which are in the middle of the floor, where he had dropped them when the lights went off.

He pushes them across the floor to MARIYA.

FELIKS: Take the truck. Get out of here.

MARIYA: Will you go with me?

FELIKS: What?

MARIYA: I'm not a great driver! And anyhow, I'm scared…

FELIKS: *NO!*

MARIYA: I'm sorry… Just drive out to the road with me…

FELIKS: *No!*

MARIYA: Okay, okay…

FELIKS: The police said they'd be back, and if I'm not here when they get here, they're gonna *look for me.*

(Beat; he remembers something.)

Aw fuck… Aw *fuck*…

MARIYA: *(Alarmed.) What?!*

FELIKS: *(Grabs the diary.)* Take this with you… I don't even know why I have it…

The police will come back, search this place, and if they find this... I don't know, I don't want it.

MARIYA: *I* don't want it!

FELIKS: I'm giving you a fucking truck! Take the book, will you?

MARIYA: OKAY!

Okay...

Headlights of car beam through the window. A car, pulling in the driveway...

FELIKS: Police... They're here... Go. Go... The back door... Please... get out of here.

MARIYA rushes out the back door. FELIKS stands up. He stares at the front door... A loud knocking on the door...

SCENE 3. FATE – 1937 – MOSCOW

NIKOLAI's living room. He is pouring wine for ISAAC and himself.

NIKOLAI: … When the police come, to your house, when they pound that door and demand entrance, what do you do? I'm asking you, this isn't some pomp-literary-rhetorical question, Isaac Babel, what do you do when the police come and pound on the door?

ISAAC: I open it?

NIKOLAI: Exactly. That is precisely what you do, you open it. Because if you don't, we will break it down. And don't bother with the back door, we already have men there waiting. You see, we have thought ahead.

ISAAC: It seems so.

NIKOLAI: And then, once the door is open, then what? Police are standing in your living room, what do you do then?

NIKOLAI stands holding both glasses of wine, but doesn't hand ISAAC his glass.

ISAAC: Offer them a drink?

NIKOLAI: *(Hadn't thought of that; still doesn't offer the drink.)* Well, we wouldn't say no–although some might think it's a bribe.

ISAAC: It's just good hospitality.

NIKOLAI: I'm trying to tell you about protocol.

ISAAC: Say I offered them a drink.

NIKOLAI: These are working men, after all, they deserve a drink.

ISAAC: Or tea.

NIKOLAI: If it's the morning.

ISAAC: They would come in the morning?

NIKOLAI: NKVD comes at all hours!

ISAAC: Morning is not so good for me.

NIKOLAI: We give no consideration to your personal whim! When police come, police come!

ISAAC: But Chief of the NKVD, Joseph Stalin's bulldog can't massage the works?

NIKOLAI: *(Laughs, finally hands ISAAC wine.)* Bulldog! That's good.
Sometimes this business happens quick and word might not reach me in time. This is why I'm briefing you – in case I can't intercede. You're my old friend, and I'll always do what I can, but justice is swift.
Also stay out of trouble and don't write anything subversive.

ISAAC: What does "subversive" mean?

NIKOLAI: You're the writer, you tell me.

ISAAC: It always means something different to someone else.

NIKOLAI: It means what it means. I didn't invite you over here to just drink wine.

ISAAC: I was wondering. It's been a long time.

NIKOLAI: To warn you. Things are going to become very difficult for writers.

ISAAC: What writers?

NIKOLAI: All writers. Especially creative type writers like you.

ISAAC: Very difficult how?

NIKOLAI: Just stay out of trouble and don't write anything subversive.

ISAAC: Okay, and then?

NIKOLAI: Then, this is the most important part of everything. Remember this over anything else I ever tell you. Are you listening?

ISAAC: Yes.

NIKOLAI: Never confess.

ISAAC: Never confess what?

NIKOLAI: What did I just say!? Never confess! You need me to translate into your dirty Odessan street talk? Never confess! Doesn't matter what, never confess!

ISAAC: Okay. "Never confess". So lie?

NIKOLAI: I didn't say that I just said "never confess". Even if they torture you.

ISAAC: *(Almost laughing.)* They're going to torture me?

NIKOLAI: NEVER CONFESS.

ISAAC: Okay. Good advice.

NIKOLAI: It's good to see you, it's been too long.

ISAAC: Here's to your promotion.

NIKOLAI: No, here's to your fame and fortune.

ISAAC: Here's to the shit wine of Poland.

NIKOLAI: Here's to your stinking, miserable lies.

ISAAC: I've never told a lie ever. I categorically deny the accusation.

They laugh and drink.

NIKOLAI: Wait! Do you want cakes?

ISAAC: No thank you.

NIKOLAI: You don't like cakes?

ISAAC: I like cakes.

NIKOLAI: *(Shouting out of the room.) Yevgenia! Bring cakes!*

(To ISAAC.)

My wife.

(Shouts.)

Yevgenia!
She sits in there all day, reading, like a mouse.

ISAAC: Nikolai, I do not need any cakes, I assure you, I...

He stops when he sees YEVGENIA standing in the door. She looks at ISAAC, and he stands up, dumbfounded by her beauty.

NIKOLAI: Yes, good, Yevgenia! This is my old friend from the war in Poland. I've told you of him.

YEVGENIA: Isaac Babel. Stories and poems and screenplays! My husband speaks of you often.

NIKOLAI: No I do not speak of him often.

YEVGENIA: Forgive me – not often – but he speaks of you... he speaks of you with great fondness.

NIKOLAI: No I do not.

ISAAC: Madam, I am enchanted to meet you.

He kisses her hand.

NIKOLAI: *(As he exits; annoyed.)* I will fetch the cakes, I will get them, I must do everything around this miserable house...

NIKOLAI is gone. YEVGENIA and ISAAC look at each other, both entranced by the other.

YEVGENIA: You wrote a film! What is that like?

ISAAC: It's remarkable, you know. To watch your own deepest notions come alive across a screen.

YEVGENIA: That seems rather terrifying, actually.

ISAAC: In my experience... What is terrifying can be thrilling.

YEVGENIA: I suppose... yes...

(Changing subject.)

I have always dreamed about what it might be like to be in a film.

ISAAC: Well then, let's arrange that. You could be in *my* film.

YEVGENIA: What do you… NO!

NIKOLAI enters with cakes.

ISAAC: Nikolai, don't you think so?

NIKOLAI: What?

ISAAC: Yevgenia should act in my film.

NIKOLAI: *(As if this is the funniest thing he's ever heard.)* Ha! Ha! Yes, that's good, that's perfect!

ISAAC: You could, you could!

YEVGENIA: But I am not an actress…

ISAAC: Nikolai… You've told me yourself, haven't you? Your wife is very talented.

NIKOLAI: She's okay.

ISAAC: Let us cast you then! A starlet of the silver screen!

YEVGENIA: Don't be silly…!

NIKOLAI: Babel… Wives are not actresses, wives are wives.

YEVGENIA: Isaac Babel, are you married?

ISAAC: *(Awkwardly.)* Yes.

This news is surprising to NIKOLAI. He gets angrier than he should, as if he's been lied to.

NIKOLAI: *WHAT?* You married!? When did you marry?

ISAAC: Nine years ago.

NIKOLAI: Nine years!?

You never told me you were married! You never told me that! You didn't invite me to your wedding!

YEVGENIA: Dear...

NIKOLAI: No!

Is this one of your stupid lies again?

ISAAC: I'm afraid I am married.

NIKOLAI: *(Forceful to ISAAC.)* Why wouldn't you tell me you were married?

ISAAC: It's not something I speak about.

She lives in Paris and...

NIKOLAI: *(The weirdest thing he has ever heard.) Your wife lives in Paris?*

ISAAC: Yes. And I live here. In Moscow.

NIKOLAI: Why does your wife live in *Paris?*

ISAAC: Yevgenia, have you been to Paris?

NIKOLAI & YEVGENIA: No.

ISAAC: Well! Paris is...

(Beat.)

Nikolai, in Paris... there are *no rules.*

NIKOLAI: *(Hushed.) My God...*

ISAAC: Once you've been, you'll never want to leave. So she stayed.

She's happier in Paris.

And I'm happier that she's in Paris.

NIKOLAI: Oh. Well. I understand that.

ISAAC: Nikolai, many actresses are married and so they are both wives and actresses... and all I'm saying is that Yevgenia could be both, too.

YEVGENIA: That's quite enough! My husband is right: I am a wife. Besides, no actress is just cast in a role simply because the writer feels like it.

ISAAC: I mean…

YEVGENIA: Actors audition!

NIKOLAI: Yes, you see? There are specific regulations one must follow to achieve acting.

ISAAC: Then audition. For me. Right now. I will tell you what to say and then you "perform" it.

NIKOLAI loves this. His eyes go wide.

NIKOLAI: Terrific! Yes! Do this!

YEVGENIA: This is foolishness, plain and simple! I will leave you gentlemen to your jokes and wine.

NIKOLAI: Yevgenia! You don't leave this room. Audition!

(To her quietly.)

This is good fun.

He has insisted and she realizes she must. She straightens her spine, and decides to just get this over with.

YEVGENIA: Writerly mischief, is what it seems like, but yes, carry on.

ISAAC: Wonderful! You play… *Daria*. You are speaking to *Gashpar*, a man who has a briefcase with something very important inside of it. You need the briefcase, but you can't let him know that. And so you are trying to be charming. Also you are in love with him. And he loves you, but you don't know that yet.

NIKOLAI: What a character!

YEVGENIA: What's in the briefcase?

ISAAC: Information.

YEVGENIA: About what.

ISAAC: About who you are. Daria has amnesia, and she is trying to figure out who she is.

YEVGENIA: Fine. Go.

ISAAC: Gashpar is sitting on a park bench near a lake in Odessa. You walk to him.

(She does.)

Wonderful! Wonderful!

YEVGENIA: Go.

ISAAC: "There used to be more ducks in this lake."

YEVGENIA really "acts". It's overacting, but it's also kind of grand, but totally wrong for the words she's saying.

YEVGENIA: *"There used to be more ducks in this lake."*

ISAAC: Oh, that's excellent, that's very good…

(Beat.)

"But I heard they were all killed."

YEVGENIA: *"But I heard they were all killed."*

ISAAC: At which point Gashpar says:

(He performs .)

"Madam, they were not killed, they just flew away."

(Beat.)

And then she replies: "How lovely to think so."

YEVGENIA: *(Staring in ISAAC's eyes.)* *"How lovely to think so."*

ISAAC: And then he says, *"Not as lovely as your eyes."*

Brief awkward beat… she eyes ISAAC.

YEVGENIA: That's what he says?

ISAAC: That's his line.

YEVGENIA: A little hackneyed, isn't it?

ISAAC: No, it's the style of the piece. And then she sits and she says, "Do you have information for me?"

YEVGENIA: *Do you have information for me?*

ISAAC: And Gashpar replies: *I do.*
And then *Daria* says… "You remind me of someone I have known forever."

YEVGENIA: … *"You remind me of someone… I have known forever."*

ISAAC: And he says, *I AM the man who has known you forever. I am the man you have seen since you opened your eyes. It's me. Look at me. Look at me and remember.*
And then she looks at him and she says, "I remember."

YEVGENIA is suddenly nervous, uncomfortable…

But NIKOLAI is engrossed in the story… as if he can't wait to hear what happens next, and then gets impatient…

NIKOLAI: Say the *line*, Yevgenia!

YEVGENIA: This is so challenging! I'm struggling. Nikolai, you be Gashpar.

NIKOLAI: What? No.

ISAAC: He doesn't want to… Just pretend I'm Gashpar, you're doing very well.

YEVGENIA: Niki… Please be Gashpar.

ISAAC takes the hint, but is surly about it.

ISAAC: Fine, let's go back. Nikolai, say: *"Those ducks were not killed, they just flew away."*

NIKOLAI: *(As flat as possible.)* "They were not killed, they just flew away."

ISAAC: And now you ask if you may sit down.

YEVGENIA: *"May I sit?"*

ISAAC: And he says yes.

NIKOLAI: "Yes."

ISAAC: And you say, "No, the ducks were lined up and executed, each of them shot in the back of their duck heads…"

NIKOLAI: What kind of rubbish is this.

YEVGENIA: Hush, Niki.

(Now she addresses all the lines directly to ISAAC.)

"No, the ducks were lined up and executed, each of them shot in the back of their duck heads…"

ISAAC: "By other duck gangsters."

YEVGENIA: *"By other duck gangsters".*

NIKOLAI: WHAT KIND OF RUBBISH IS THIS?!

ISAAC: *(Starts to get carried away with the story.)*

"The duck gangsters rule this town of Odessa and they have either killed the other ducks or put them to work in illegal black markets, which is why the price of eggs is so high, also because the ducks have arrested all the chickens." But then Gashpar says, "But those are chicken eggs." And then you say…

YEVGENIA: That's too many words…

ISAAC: Nevermind, and then Gashpar says, "don't I know you?" Say it, Nikolai.

NIKOLAI: "Don't I know you?"

ISAAC: And she says, "You don't know me, but I know you."

YEVGENIA: *"You don't know me, but I know you."*

ISAAC: And he says, "Don't talk about ducks. There are no more ducks."

NIKOLAI: *(Eating cake.)* "Don't talk about ducks. There are no more ducks."

ISAAC: And then she reaches into her coat pocket and pulls out a baby duck.

NIKOLAI: *(With disproportionate rage; spitting cake.)* This is *bullshit!* This story makes *no sense!* What ducks!? Nothing you're saying is making any sense!

YEVGENIA: Niki—

NIKOLAI: NO! No No No NO! I told you nothing subversive.

YEVGENIA: Darling, that's not subversive!

NIKOLAI: You don't even know what that word means, Yevgenia!

YEVGENIA: It means *against the rules.*

NIKOLAI: Exactly! *That's* what it means! And I told you *Nothing Subversive!*

ISAAC: There is nothing subversive about a duck.

NIKOLAI: Yes! *Gangster* ducks are subversive!

ISAAC: But not baby ducks.
Not baby ducks, Nikolai.

For a moment NIKOLAI is silenced by this air-tight logic.

NIKOLAI: You listen to me, you fool! The world is about to change and I'm trying to warn you! Why can't you... why can't you... *SEE?!*

ISAAC: See what? The future?

NIKOLAI: *Yes.*

ISAAC: Could Yevgenia tell us? Couldn't she tell us what will happen?

YEVGENIA is subtly exasperated; has had enough with ISAAC's games.

NIKOLAI: What?

ISAAC: Yevgenia... you can see the future, isn't that true?

YEVGENIA: What nonsense.

NIKOLAI: *(To ISAAC.)* How do you know about that?

ISAAC: You told me.

NIKOLAI: I told you what?

ISAAC: The night we met.

NIKOLAI: I don't remember the night we met!

ISAAC: Of course you do...

NIKOLAI: Unlikely. Too much memory makes a man weak.

(Proud.)

I take care to forget what is useless.

ISAAC: It was some starry night in Poland, outside of
Zhitomir... Chilly, but not too cold, although you could
see your breath... or maybe we were smoking... But I had
stolen wine from a cathedral, and we drank it together, and
you showed me Venus in the Eastern sky, and told me of
your wife, whom you loved, and who knew of such things
as planets and stars and constellations and the peculiarities
of fate.
She could tell the future, he told me.
She could tell men's fortunes.
Would you tell me my fortune?
Nikolai is telling me I must be worried about the future.
But I hate worrying!
Please... Tell me if I should worry. Or if I can relieve
myself of that weary task.

YEVGENIA: I think there have been enough games for one night.

ISAAC: Nikolai, don't you think this is a good idea?

NIKOLAI: She only predicts war.

YEVGENIA: Niki, don't be silly! I've predicted many things... I predicted your promotion, your glorious career, your long life...

ISAAC: Which you've had!

NIKOLAI: *(Hostile towards her.)* And many children. The many children we were to have.

YEVGENIA: And all these things will happen.

NIKOLAI looks at her, with a weighted hostility. Then he looks at ISAAC, who tries to get him to smile. After a moment NIKOLAI shakes his head, acquiescing...

NIKOLAI: Very well, do his fortune.

ISAAC: Excellent!

YEVGENIA: There's too much pressure now, I don't know...

NIKOLAI: Now she's timid. No. Too late. Do this.

YEVGENIA: Well, let us see... There are many ways to tell someone's fortune. I can read your furrowed brow... or the roots of your hair...
Or your palm... here, let me see your hand...

NIKOLAI: Do the one with the water! The water and the blindfolds! That's the one that works.

YEVGENIA: Niki, that's rather involved...

NIKOLAI: But that's the one that works!

YEVGENIA: Fine, we will perform a Baltic Salt-Water Forearm Scrub.

ISAAC: *(Delighted.)* What is *that?*

YEVGENIA: An old measurement of fate, mostly forgotten or disregarded.
It requires materials...

NIKOLAI: *(As if he has to do everything around here.)* I will get them, I will fetch them, this isn't complicated!

He leaves. ISAAC and YEVGENIA stare at each other.

A beat. She's not happy with him…

YEVGENIA: Maybe Paris is a better place for a man like you.

ISAAC: Not me. I'm a Russian man.

YEVGENIA: But there are no rules in Paris, yes? And you are not a man who loves rules and…

(Beat.)

Why do you say to me… the things that you say to me? Are you mad?

Do you understand what he can do to you?!

ISAAC: Yezhov brought me here tonight because he cares about me.

YEVGENIA: You don't know him.

He comes home stained with blood. Every day I make sure his uniform is clean and pressed.

You don't know what goes on out there…

(With pity.)

You're just a writer.

ISAAC: Do you like that I'm a writer?

YEVGENIA: I don't care.

ISAAC: Have you ever stood on the edge of a cliff where one step forward would send you hurtling down to your death?

YEVGENIA: I live in Moscow, so, *no.*

(Beat.)

I don't care about your writing or movies or being in movies. Or carrying on about someone's eyes and what they might look like.

I don't care about being in love. Or ducks.

(Beat.)

Or baby ducks.

NIKOLAI enters with a basin and a cloth and some colorful scarves.

YEVGENIA: Okay.

Let's set up this table. I will sit here, Isaac, across from me, and Niki, there. We sit together. We put on blindfolds.

NIKOLAI: I'm not wearing a blindfold.

YEVGENIA: You have to for it to work.

NIKOLAI: I'm not wearing a blindfold.

YEVGENIA: You have to.

NIKOLAI: Why.

YEVGENIA: It's the rules.

NIKOLAI sits down and puts a blindfold on. He picks up his wine and continues drinking.

YEVGENIA: Isaac, roll up your sleeves past your elbows.

He does. She sets up the basin, and puts the cloth in the water,

YEVGENIA: Now blindfold yourself. And I will blindfold myself and I will wash your forearms. And I will tell you your future.

They solemnly blindfold themselves.

NIKOLAI: *(Annoyed.)* Everything is black!

YEVGENIA squeezes and wrings out the cloth.

She holds the squeezed cloth over one of ISAAC's forearms. As drops of water fall on his arm, we hear an amplified sound of dripping…

which morphs into drips with a heartbeat, and a pulse of some rhythmic music as YEVGENIA washes one forearm thoroughly.

It's intimate, tender, and then gains in force. She periodically puts the cloth back in the basin, taking less and less time to wring it out, and doing it with more intensity, so water starts to get everywhere.

She cleans both arms, probing them, as if searching for something. She alternates between the two arms, and between a fierce scrubbing and a soft, caress...

As it gets more frenzied, the music increases... and then suddenly it stops as YEVGENIA throws the cloth in the basin hard and rips off her blindfold and stares at ISAAC... in horror and sadness.

YEVGENIA: There is nothing but war ahead.

(Beat.)

You have only three years to live.

She lets go of his hand, quietly stands up and walks away, troubled and disturbed by the vision she just had. ISAAC takes off his blindfold and looks at her. He gets up and walks to her. NIKOLAI remains seated, oblivious, drinking his wine.

The scene shifts into...

Transition:

ISAAC and YEVGENIA kiss. NIKOLAI disappears. ISAAC helps YEVGENIA age. She becomes much older. Her hair becomes grey.

YEVGENIA ages fifty-two years before our eyes. But not ISAAC, who remains young, and then steps away from YEVGENIA, who is now in her eighties. ISAAC watches her fade from sight.

Elsewhere, VOVA, thirties, serious, imposing, strong, wearing a cheap suit, stands in an elevator, descending deep underground...

SCENE 4. BUREAU 42 – 1989 – MOSCOW

The elevator doors open. VOVA enters Bureau 42, a vast underground office. An archive. It is filled entirely with files carefully, manically, organized on shelves that go on forever. The files are old, dusty, decrepit. But well organized.

In the midst of the archive is one desk, empty except for a ledger, a fountain pen and a bell.

VOVA looks as if he has never been here. He looks around. He taps the bell on the desk. It rings.

NIKOLAI Yezhov, now in his nineties, shuffles from out of the mountains of information, as if he had been a beast camouflaged by his natural habitat.

NIKOLAI: Who rings my bell?

VOVA: Me sir. I was summoned.

NIKOLAI: You were summoned by whom?

VOVA: Fifth Chief Directorate, by proxy of 9th Deputy Directorate, by proxy of 27th Operational Collegium Assistant Deputy Directorate.

NIKOLAI: So you are the Dresden man.

VOVA: Yes sir. Sub-Deputy Directorate S.

NIKOLAI: What is your accent?

VOVA: Standard Russian. Straight across the middle.

NIKOLAI: No. Nothing is straight across the middle. Nothing is standard.
Your accent: Leningrad.
Leningrad, yes?

VOVA: Yes sir.

NIKOLAI: What is your cover?

VOVA: Translator and interpreter.

NIKOLAI: How is your German.

VOVA: Good enough.

NIKOLAI: Don't say "Good enough" say "Good". Phrasing of the truth is vital.

VOVA: Yes sir.

NIKOLAI: When we say that something is true, it becomes true. When we say that something is false, it becomes false.

(Beat.)

How is your German?

VOVA: "Good".

NIKOLAI: Good! How is Dresden?

VOVA: "Good".

NIKOLAI: Good! How is KGB?

VOVA: "Good".

NIKOLAI: Is it clear now how this works?

VOVA: Yes sir.

NIKOLAI: Good!

Awkward, long beat, as NIKOLAI makes his way to his chair and slowly eases his way down.

NIKOLAI: Sit.

There's no chair for VOVA.

There's a chair over there.

VOVA goes amid some files and finds a very small chair, too small for him. But he has no choice except to sit in it.

NIKOLAI: The Dresden Man! From Leningrad.
Your *friends...* call you "Vova".
Ah, you are surprised I know your nickname. Nicknames! I like them. I will call you "Vova".

VOVA: Yes sir.

NIKOLAI: Yezhov, N. N stands for Nikolai.

VOVA: Yes sir, I know who you are, Yezhov Comrade, sir.

NIKOLAI: First Chief Directorate, Level Double 'A' and *Chairman* of Bureau 42.

(He gestures to the files around them.)

Have you ever been to Bureau 42, young Vova?

VOVA: No, Yezhov Comrade.

NIKOLAI: That is because it is Top Secret and you don't have clearance! There's a lot of censorship within the Soviet government, yes?

VOVA: *Censorship?*

NIKOLAI: Every story that is told, officially, from the state, has been sheared and shaped, some might say *distorted*, and ultimately changed.
But all that information—everything that's cut away and struck from the record? It all ends up down here. Here in Bureau 42, we have the history of the Soviet Union. The real history. This endless lair, sixty-five meters beneath the streets of Moscow is a repository for The Truth. Unvarnished, untrammelled, *truth*.
In *addition to that*, the KGB, or before that, the NKVD, have been spying on hundreds of millions of people since 1917, and every document, every last note scribbled on a napkin is down here, carefully documented and filed away.

As he talks, NIKOLAI pulls a drawer out from a cabinet... a drawer that is impossibly long, it continues to roll out, far longer than any realistic drawer might be... from this he takes a sizeable file out.

NIKOLAI: I have the history of half the world down here. What do you think about that?

VOVA: I suppose that is "Good".

NIKOLAI: Test me.

VOVA: Yezhov Comrade… I believe you…

NIKOLAI waves the file at VOVA.

NIKOLAI: This is *your* file, Sub-Directorate S! Your entire life is in here! *Test me!*

(Flips through it; skimming it.)

How many times have you broken your nose?

VOVA: What?

NIKOLAI: Your nose! How many times has it been broken?

VOVA: I don't know…

NIKOLAI: Twelve times! *Twelve times*! Poor Vova! Schoolyard bullies.

VOVA: That's not how my nose was broken!

NIKOLAI: Then how?

VOVA: Doing sport.

NIKOLAI: Doing what sport?

VOVA: Doing judo.

NIKOLAI: *Doing judo.* Okay.

NIKOLAI takes out a black magic marker and opens VOVA's file and crosses something out. Then writes something…

NIKOLAI: *"Doing… Judo…"*
Now your file has been adjusted. It said here you were bullied, now there is no mention of bullies.
Now there is "judo".

(Beat.)

Do you understand what that means?
Respond please: Yes, No.

VOVA: Yes.

NIKOLAI: What does it mean?

VOVA: It means… When you say that something is true it becomes true.

NIKOLAI: *(He waves the magic marker like a wand.)* Behold, Young Vladimir: The Black Magic Marker: The most useful tool in all of communism. There is nothing that cannot be eventually crossed out, and changed…

(Beat.)

I understand you wish to be assigned to deep cover in the United States.

VOVA: Yes sir, very much.

NIKOLAI: This is your "dream".

VOVA: Very much Yezhov Comrade.

NIKOLAI: I don't trust agents who "dream" for the United States because, naturally, I assume they are treacherous and intend to defect. Is this your intention?

VOVA: Yezhov Comrade, no, absolutely not.

NIKOLAI: Why do you "dream", then, for America?

VOVA: That is where the fight is. I am a man who goes towards a fight, not away.

NIKOLAI: How has that worked out for you and your nose?

VOVA: I will let a man break my nose if I might break his skull.

NIKOLAI: A blunt strategy, but yes, okay: effective.

VOVA: I would never defect! When we bury them, Yezhov Comrade, I will be holding a shovel.

NIKOLAI is taken aback.

NIKOLAI: You will be holding a what?

VOVA: I will be holding a shovel.

Awkward beat, before NIKOLAI goes back into VOVA's file.

NIKOLAI: I have a job for you. Carry it out expeditiously, and you will receive a transfer to your post of choice.

VOVA: That is… That's very good… Sir, that's… "Good." "Good."

NIKOLAI: But wait! I am not convinced that I can trust you.

VOVA: You can trust me!

NIKOLAI: *(Imitates him.) You can trust me!*
Leningrad accent! Coarse. It is the dialect of thugs, which is what you sound like to me: a thug.

VOVA: I am not a thug.

NIKOLAI: *(Reading his file.)* How can I be so sure? This file states that while attending KGB academy, you received fifteen citations of insubordination.

VOVA: That's not true!

NIKOLAI: It's clearly notated. Fifteen citations.

VOVA: Not once. Not once was I insubordinate.

NIKOLAI: Fine.

NIKOLAI crosses out another section of the file.

NIKOLAI: *"Never… insubordinate…"*

(Reads.)

You were born in Moscow?

VOVA: No! Leningrad!

NIKOLAI: But here: States: Place of birth: Moscow.

VOVA: It's wrong. Again, it's wrong!

NIKOLAI uses the magic marker again, crosses out, writes.

NIKOLAI: *(Reads; surprised.)* You were born in a brothel?

VOVA: That's… No, that's absurd.

NIKOLAI: *(Reads.)* "To a brothel in Moscow he was born."

VOVA: It's a lie!

NIKOLAI: *(Not reading; looking at VOVA.)* So your mother was a whore!

Awkward, tense beat. VOVA changes; this is unacceptable.

NIKOLAI: I say: Your mother: A whore.

VOVA: When I was eight years old I threw a brick at a man's head because he swore at my mother, for no reason, in the middle of the street. I wanted to kill him, but I missed his head and the brick hit his neck instead, and crushed his voice box. He was never able to speak above a whisper after that. This is the thing I am most proud of in my life. That I took away a man's voice.

(Beat.)

Is *that* in my file?

NIKOLAI: You're a reckless little shit, aren't you, Vova?

VOVA: I love my momma.

NIKOLAI: Vova loves his momma! Why don't you ask me about the rumors?

VOVA: What rumors?

NIKOLAI: *(Exasperated; this should be obvious.) The rumors about your mother!*

VOVA: I don't believe rumors, rumors are lies.

(Beat; uneasy.)

What rumors?

NIKOLAI: Nobody remembers you before the age of five.

Nobody remembers your mother being pregnant.
Your parents are both frail and skinny and small. You are not.
People in your neighborhood remember a woman bringing a child to the building one night, but the facts are clouded and dim.

(Beat.)

You have spent your entire life wondering if your parents are your parents. If your mother is your mother.

VOVA: None of that is true.

NIKOLAI: Are you calling me a liar?

VOVA: No, but...

NIKOLAI: Because I am calling *you* a liar.
You have always wondered these things, and I know you have, because you wrote about it in a notebook once when you were sixteen years old, an adolescent epic screed of how you wondered if your real mother left you in a basket on a river like Moses.

From VOVA's file, NIKOLAI holds up a crumpled, torn-and-taped-together old piece of notebook paper.

He hands it to VOVA who takes it.

VOVA: I didn't...
How do you...?
I didn't write this.

(Beat; he says it with more authority.)

I did not write that.

NIKOLAI points to a photo of him standing with Stalin.

NIKOLAI: I used to stand by Stalin's side! His right hand man! His chief of police!
But then I was erased!

He takes out an identical photo, but now there is only Stalin there, no NIKOLAI.

NIKOLAI: I was removed from every official photo the government has...

They proclaimed me dead, buried in a mass grave with the enemies of the state!

But did I die? Was I erased? Answer!

VOVA: No...

NIKOLAI: No! I remain! Through the force of my own will.

I exist.

I reclaimed the truth.

And now I control the truth.

(Beat.)

As for you...

In this file, young Vova, are things you have wondered about your whole life.

Terrible secrets.

Unfathomable gossip. Rumors.

Would you like to know it?

Would you like to read it?

Or would you state the truth about yourself... I can, I will make those changes for you *right now*.

Read *this*. Or dictate.

Choose one.

NIKOLAI holds out the file for VOVA to read. He stares at it. It seems to glow, to beckon... every answer to every important question he ever had.

He considers and then he turns away, faces forward like a good soldier.

VOVA: I was born in Leningrad, in the wake of a siege.

My brothers: dead.

My uncles: dead.

My aunts: dead

Everyone except my parents.

… My mother is good, is decent… My mother… is my mother.

NIKOLAI crosses out large swaths of VOVA's file with the magic marker. VOVA watches, then continues.

VOVA: I am a field agent for *KGB*.

My record is impeccable.

I have never been insubordinate.

I am expert at judo.

NIKOLAI: *Expert.*

VOVA: It is said…

It has been said that…

(Beat.)

I am a good man.

NIKOLAI: Good and not good, these are not considerations.
But everything else…

(He scratches, writes.)

Yes.

NIKOLAI continues to systematically cross every line out of the file. As he does it, VOVA looks over, watching his history become erased. As NIKOLAI works at this, he speaks…

NIKOLAI: I like you, 19th Sub-Deputy Directorate S. And I like your brutish Leningrad accent, and I like that you hail from the streets of that city, and I like that you're a thug. Embrace your thuggish roots.

Be who you are and you might rise high in tomorrow's Soviet Union.

When the world is a gang fight, people want a gangster to lead them.

VOVA: Yes Yezhov Comrade.

NIKOLAI puts the file back into the long file cabinet drawer and shuts it.

NIKOLAI: I have a grand-daughter.

> She lives in Dresden, and like so many rootless youth, she longs for the West.
>
> She is attempting to defect to West Berlin.
>
> This must not happen.

VOVA: When did you last see her?

NIKOLAI: I have never seen her.

> *(Beat.)*
>
> You are to place her under surveillance, and ensure that she does not leave East Germany. But listen to me: *she is not to be arrested.* You are simply to contain her. Succeed and I will place you in deep cover within the United States.

VOVA: I will do everything you ask of me.

NIKOLAI gives him a file.

NIKOLAI: This is her file.

> *NIKOLAI takes out a box and from the box takes out enormous 1980's era headphones, with way too many wires coming out of them, that seem impossibly long...*

NIKOLAI: And these! These are *new*. Developed by top engineers.

> They hear... *everything.*
>
> *VOVA puts on the headphones. First he hears delicate sounds... dripping, an echo of something, the plucking of strings or bristling of a broom...*
>
> *URZULA appears, sweeping and humming to herself...*
>
> *Music joins her... and she begins to sing... casually at first, but growing in confidence until it ends in a true performance.*

URZULA: Somewhere In The Milky Way
Fading With The Light Of Day...
Shines A Morning Star...
So Blue...

Lower In The Eastern Sky
You Can See Me Floating By...
I Can See You Too...

Alone And Lost
In Outer Space:
You Know My Name...
I Know Your Face...

High! In The Cosmic Blue!
I'm Falling!
I'm Falling...
To You...

End of Act I.

Act II

URZULA sits at the kitchen table. Her suitcase by her side. It's late in the evening. She has a drink. She's in despair.

She goes into her suitcase, shuffles through it, finds Babel's diary.

She opens it. Begins reading.

ISAAC appears elsewhere, as he did in 1920, in the Red Cavalry. But he speaks to URZULA, who reads...

ISAAC: If only some government or other were a kind one.

    (Beat.)

    Describe the market, baskets of cherries, interior of cookshop. Conversation with a Russian woman who came to borrow a washtub. Sweat, anemic tea. I'm beginning to get my teeth into life.

URZULA turns the page, reads something else.

ISAAC: Describe the family – beautiful wife, husband, carrying child. Market in Zhitomir.
Synagogue buildings, ancient architecture, how deeply it all moves me.
I'm tired.
And suddenly I'm lonely.
Life flows past me, and what does it mean...?

She shuts the book, and she begins to weep. She makes no sound, but her eyes well up. ISAAC looks at her, kindly. And then he leaves.

YEVGENIA enters, having just woken up, still groggy. But sturdy.

YEVGENIA: Zula...! Zula, what is going on, why are you up so late in the night here!

URZULA: It's not so late Babcia... I was reading...

YEVGENIA: She's crying! Why is my Zula crying?

URZULA dries her tears, YEVGENIA picks up Babel's diary.

YEVGENIA: This book makes Zula cry?

URZULA: No...

YEVGENIA: Then what? Have you eaten dinner?

(Gasps at this criminal oversight.)

You haven't eaten dinner!
And now, *look!*
You sit here, I'll make something to eat.

YEVGENIA starts puttering around the kitchen.

URZULA: I'm not hungry, Babcia.

YEVGENIA: That's okay, I'll re-heat this Qureshi.

URZULA: Ugh, we are not eating Qureshi.

YEVGENIA: Why not?
Can't sleep? Qureshi.
Bad thoughts? Qureshi.
Crying? Qureshi.
What else?

URZULA: Want to throw up? Qureshi.

YEVGENIA: You sit here and drink brandy.

(Pours her a drink; addresses the elephant in room.)

So! Zula is still here. When Babcia kissed you goodnight, you were going to leave. Suitcase packed! But here you are, still here, still not left.

URZULA: I'm not leaving.

YEVGENIA: Zula-la-la... You are a dreaming girl...

URZULA: No...

YEVGENIA: … You dream and dream and dream. But you must go! If you don't go to the West you will be sad, sadder than you are now.

URZULA: I'm not sad, I'm happy.

YEVGENIA: She has a routine: She makes plans, she finds a man to take her to the West, and then she gets scared and stops cold.

URZULA: I don't want to leave.

YEVGENIA: Look at me, Zula.

URZULA: *What?*

YEVGENIA: Opportunities: *Infrequent.*

URZULA: I know.

YEVGENIA: How many more chances will she get?

If an opportunity comes again, you take it in your teeth this time.

URZULA: I can't leave you. I can't leave you here alone.

YEVGENIA: Zula, when you leave me, I will miss you so much, but I will also have this nice big apartment to myself, and I have so many ideas what to do. First thing: Bookshelves! Too many books strewn around!

URZULA laughs, in spite of everything.

URZULA: Everyone used to be braver.

(More to herself; but YEVGENIA listens.)

When I read this diary, I think of him, the awful things he lives through, and yet he writes, he writes everything down. He's compassionate! He's enraged! The misery of the world, and here's me, stuck, too frightened to even step outside and possibly *do* something.

I wish I was more like you and him, Babcia.

Brave and smart.

YEVGENIA: Can't be both! Choose one!

URZULA: I'm neither.

YEVGENIA: *(She sits, pours a drink for herself.)* It's unpleasant, leaving is, yes?

URZULA: Saying goodbye to you forever? Yes, that's unpleasant.

YEVGENIA: So we say goodbye! Maybe forever, maybe not. This is the case with all goodbyes.

(Beat.)

If you want something… an unpleasantness is required first. That's the rules!

So I don't want to hear this excuse anymore.

You are simply afraid. Give me your hand.

URZULA does. YEVGENIA studies it.

YEVGENIA: Yep. See? The path to the West is filled with unpleasantness.

(Beat.)

Also, there is nothing but war ahead.

A knocking at the door. Insistent, authoritative. URZULA tenses, she quickly takes Babel's diary and puts it back in her suitcase.

Knocking stops. Knocking starts again. URZULA goes to the door and opens it. VOVA is there.

URZULA: Yes? May I help you?

VOVA: Urzula Solomonovna?

URZULA: Yes.

VOVA: I would like to speak to you.

URZULA: About what? Who are you?

VOVA: May I come in?

She quiets, backs away, to let him in. He comes in. He takes in the room.

YEVGENIA: Zula, who is this man?

VOVA: Good evening, Mum. I am here to speak to your daughter.

YEVGENIA: *(Flattered.)* My *daughter*. You are a sweet man. She's my grand-daughter! My daughter is dead, she had the cancer.

VOVA: *(To URZULA.)* You are taking a trip!

URZULA: What?

VOVA: *(Points.)* Suitcase. Taking a trip somewhere?

YEVGENIA: That's dirty laundry boy. Unless you want to get to work washing, don't go kicking around near that.

VOVA: *(To URZULA.)* May I sit down?

URZULA: What is it you want, sir?

VOVA: I want to sit down. May I do that?

YEVGENIA: Sit! Sit! Such formalities with young people these days. We are eating soup, you'll eat soup too, yes? Qureshi.

URZULA: *Babcia, he doesn't want any Qureshi.*

VOVA: No, that sounds lovely, Mum, thank you. I would love to have soup with you.

URZULA: What do you want, sir? I'm sure you didn't come over here to eat dinner with us.

VOVA: No, I didn't. But your *Babcia* just extended a courtesy. And I am hungry.

(Beat.)

But first a story! Two men and two women… were arrested this evening by an undercover police officer. They were attempting to flee to the West.

(Beat.)

I spoke to each of them, individually.
In speaking to them, and explaining to them the
consequences for their illegal action, two people provided
your name. They said you were part of their plan. The
other two lied so as to not implicate you.

(Beat.)

Are you trying to escape to the West, Urzula?

YEVGENIA: Qureshi is almost ready. Doesn't it smell good?

VOVA: No.

YEVGENIA: Smells bad?

VOVA: *No!* It doesn't smell one way or the other, Mum,
I'm speaking to your –

YEVGENIA: Ohhhh… You got no sense of *smell!*

VOVA: I can too.

YEVGENIA: You can't smell things!

VOVA: It's a common condition.

YEVGENIA: *(As if this makes him less of a man.)* I never met a
man who couldn't smell.

VOVA: *(Defensive.)* I operate fine.

YEVGENIA: You're a handicapped.

VOVA: I am not a handicapped person, I merely can't smell,
because of sport, because of judo.

YEVGENIA: Got bullied!

VOVA: I didn't get bullied! I was a champion. Enough!

(To URZULA.)

Urzula, you don't have to tell me anything, I already know
you are trying to escape.

I could arrest you right now, but I am electing not to.
And so you are not in prison with your friends.

(Beat.)

By the way...
It was the men who mentioned your name. The women
lied to try to save you.
Or was it the other way around?
Who did what? What is true? What is not true?

(Beat; as if to definitively answer.)

It was the men. The men said your name to me. The women
were loyal to you.
And so they lied to us, to save you. And so they paid a
dear price for their lies, which is what happens to all liars.

(Beat.)

"Loyalty" is volatile.
You must know where to put it... so that it does not one
day explode in your face.

URZULA: I haven't don't anything wrong. I didn't ever leave
my home. I'm *here*.

VOVA: But you don't want to be. I am here because I am kind.
I am giving you advice. And the best advice I can give
you, for your general life, is do not try to escape *any more*.
You will hurt people along the way.
[URZULA: Please!]
And yourself.
And you will not succeed. I can guarantee you this. I will
contain you.

YEVGENIA brings soup to table.

YEVGENIA: Now we eat, come, come eat Qureshi.

VOVA: *(Quietly to URZULA; friendly.)* Let's eat!

YEVGENIA: Zula, come! You need to eat!

URZULA, although it's the last thing she wants to do, joins them at the table.

YEVGENIA and URZULA, as if second nature, take needles and prick their fingers, a couple of fingers on each hand and then dip their fingers in the soup.

VOVA: What is that? What are you doing. Are those needles?

YEVGENIA: You need to feed them.

VOVA: *(Looking in the soup.)* Are those...?

(He stirs; sees; freaks out.)

Those are *leeches...*

URZULA: Yes.

VOVA: They're alive.

URZULA: It's a Polish soup.

VOVA: – They are sucking your blood.

YEVGENIA takes his hand and pricks his fingers...

VOVA: Ow!

YEVGENIA: *Ow* he says.

YEVGENIA takes VOVA's hand and pricks two more fingers quickly.

VOVA: OW! What are you *doing!*

YEVGENIA: *You have to feed them.*

They all sit with their fingers soaking in the soup.

VOVA's face reflects how one must look the first time they've ever done this sort of thing. He may throw up.

VOVA: Is this real?

YEVEGNIA: They feast upon you... and then you feast upon them...

URZULA: *(Begrudgingly finishes the joke.)* ... *Like children.*

YEVGENIA: *(Laughing, this is an old joke.)* Like children! HA!

(To VOVA.)

Do you get this joke!? Because the infant sucks the teat and then the meddlesome parent sucks dry the will of the child to live! HA! Give and take. Do you get this joke?

VOVA: *(Hushed.) Oh God, no...!*

(Quietly; based on the leeches.) Aaggh!

YEVGENIA: Do you get this joke?

VOVA: No, I don't get the joke!

YEVGENIA: Ah, well, if you have to explain it, what's the point?

(Beat.)

Now red pepper.

She takes a teaspoon of some red pepper and sprinkles it in their bowls. They stir their soups.

YEVGENIA: They will die soon.

VOVA: The leeches die?

URZULA: Their bodies swell with blood until they burst. Then they drown in their own blood while the red pepper burns their flesh.

YEVGENIA: This is my *favorite soup.*

URZULA: Eat only a little bit. Someone who's never had Qureshi should only eat a little bit.

VOVA: I will not eat this soup.

YEVGENIA: This soup helps memory! You forgot something? *This will make you remember.*
The leeches are dead. Let's eat.

The women take their fingers out of the bowl. On each of the three pricked fingers are large, bulbous, swollen leeches.

Using their spoons, they pluck the leeches off their fingers.

The leeches plop into the soup.

They stir their soups and look at VOVA.

He tentatively does the same thing, but it is one of the most unnerving experiences of his entire life.

The women begin to eat their soup with spoons.

This appeals to him; he begins eating his soup with a spoon. A tentative and tiny sip, followed by a bigger one, a bigger one...

VOVA likes it so much that, after a moment, he puts his spoon down and holds the bowl to his face, slurping.

URZULA: Not too much! I told you! Babcia!

When VOVA's done, he puts the bowl down and stares straight ahead, as if waking from a dream. He begins to experience something akin to hallucinatory visions.

VOVA: Oh... oh my God...

YEVGENIA: You see? He's about to remember something big.

VOVA: Look at her...

(A startling memory.)

She was throwing rocks.

(With each sentence, a new memory dawns upon him.)

She wasn't afraid.
She was protecting me. She was eight years old, I was four.
She was protecting me from an animal.
It was a dog.

YEVGENIA: Oh, a dog!

VOVA: Some stray dog that I thought, then, was so big! But it was scrawny.

Probably starving and so therefore aggressive around smaller people, meaning us, meaning children, somehow cornered by him.

What is it, some alleyway, with rocks on the ground.

And garbage.

And the girl is protecting me, yelling at the dog! Throwing rocks!

YEVGENIA: Yes, yes, that's very good…

VOVA: And she hit it in the snout twice, with hefty stones, but it didn't care and kept coming… and when it leapt at me, she tackled it, and it…

It bit her face.

It tore off her eye.

The dog… the dog ate her eye.

YEVGENIA & URZULA: Eeegh.

VOVA: And I screamed, and I chased that dog.

I chased that dog away.

A long beat.

URZULA: *(To YEVGENIA.)* He's had too much soup.

YEVGENIA: He'll be fine. But he shouldn't stand up.

(Yells at him.)

DON'T STAND UP!

He tries to suddenly stand, and then falls over.

YEVGENIA: Did he fall down.

URZULA: Yes, he had / too much soup…

YEVGENIA: *(Shouts at VOVA.)* / YOU HAD TOO MUCH SOUP!

He crambles to a seated position, as if trying to play off his clumsiness… but he can't stand.

VOVA: *(New memory; the most shocking.) She was my sister!*
I had a sister.

She saved me from a dog and had her eye bitten out and eaten.

And after that, I never saw her again.

I was taken somewhere else. God, it's true: *My mother is not my mother.*

Oh God.

How could I forget that?

How could I forget I had a sister…? A different mother?

I don't know anything about myself.

YEVGENIA: *(Beat.)* Well? Do we want sweets?

(Beat.)

Do we want brandy?

(Beat.)

What do we want?

(Beat.)

Do we want a bedtime story?

(Beat.)

Zula you tell it.

URZULA: I'm not telling a fucking bed time story.

YEVGENIA: Well, that kind of language isn't called for Zula.

URZULA: Sorry.

YEVGENIA: We have a guest and you say these words.

URZULA: I'm sorry.

YEVGENIA: Once upon time there was soup.
Then there was an old lady who went to bed.
Then there was Zula and a man on the floor.

And then Zula was clever and brave.
And they all lived happily ever after…

(Beat.)

The end. Time. For. Bed.

YEVGENIA exits.

VOVA: I had a sister and I forgot about her. How is that… is this real? Is my memory even real?

URZULA: Probably. Yes. No. I don't know.

VOVA: How do I know what is true?

URZULA: I don't know, I'm the worst person to determine what is true.

VOVA: Stop. Stop doing what you are doing.

URZULA: What am I *doing?*

VOVA: You think I am incapacitated, but I'm not. I am not incapacitated.

URZULA: Okay…

She tries to covertly take her suitcase away.

VOVA: What's in the suitcase?

URZULA: Nothing.

VOVA: You were packing for escape. The most important things you own…
What did you take?
What's in that suitcase. Show me.

(With threat.) Open it and show me.

She's tense, reluctant. But then opens it. Takes out clothes, tries to hide Babel's diary.

URZULA: Mostly clothes…

VOVA: Is that a book? Is that a seditious book?

URZULA: No! It's just a diary.

VOVA: You keep a diary?

URZULA: No.

VOVA: You don't keep a diary… but *voila*, here is a diary?

URZULA: It was my grandfather's.

VOVA: Let me see it.

She is hesitant. But gives him the diary.

He looks at it, flips through it. Reads some of it.

VOVA: This is unreadable.

(Beat.)

All he does is describe things.

(He tosses it aside.) Descriptions are lies.

URZULA: *(Quietly, retrieving the diary.)* Descriptions aren't lies.

VOVA: Yes they are.

URZULA: I don't agree.

VOVA: Describe something. I'll prove you're lying.

(Beat; he thinks.)

Describe… the kitchen.

URZULA stares at him, doesn't want to play this game, but does.

URZULA: The kitchen.

(Quietly to herself.)

This is crazy…

(To him.)

"The kitchen is… warm and dark".

VOVA: *Lie.*

URZULA: How is that a lie?

VOVA: It *contains* a lie.

URZULA: What's the lie?

VOVA: The lie is what you haven't said.
    That I am the person I am, and you are the person you are.
    That we just ate our own blood.
    You tell me "the kitchen is warm and dark". I say, "you are liar".
    There's so much you left out.

URZULA: Like the fact that you can't stand up.

VOVA: Or that you have been under my surveillance for the last six months.

    Beat.

URZULA: What does that… what do you mean? Is that a lie?

VOVA: *Is* that a lie?

    (Beat.)

    How well do you think I know you?

URZULA: *(Uneasy.)* You don't… You don't know me at all.

VOVA: I know what makes you laugh, I have heard you laughing.
    I know you are unhappy, I have heard your conversations.
    I have heard you sing.
    I have heard you get drunk.
    I have heard you with two different men.
    I have heard you call them by the same nickname.
    I know which one was better.

    (Beat.)

    I heard you weep once. More than once.

I hear you reading.

I hear the pages turn.

(Beat.)

I know you want more than anything to move to the West. It is your "dream".

URZULA: It's not my dream.

You don't know me.

VOVA: Oh yes: You want to be a singer. A singer in the West. *That's* your "dream".

You think you can be a singer in the West? Your voice isn't even that good.

URZULA: I have a good voice. I'm a good singer.

VOVA: It's *fine*. It's not… It doesn't make me weep with emotion.

URZULA: Do you want me to make you weep with emotion? Is that what you want?

VOVA: No.

That's not what I…

You know what I mean, I'm not talking about myself, I'm talking about you.

You won't be a professional singer, especially not in the West.

URZULA: Maybe I will.

VOVA: No, you won't.

URZULA: Maybe I *will.*

VOVA: You are naïve. You're ignorant and deluded about your own talents.

URZULA: At least I didn't forget that I have a fucking sister.

She goes to a bottle and pours herself a drink.

URZULA: *You don't even know who you are.*

And then you eat Qureshi, you eat our soup, and now you can't even move.

Who knows how long you'll be sitting there like that? An hour? All night? Forever?

Maybe I should walk out that door right now and leave you here.

Beat.

VOVA: You are a good singer.

I listen to you sing when you clean and I…

You are good.

(Beat.)

What I am saying is I almost weep but then I don't, and so this is a fault with you, in your singing.

URZULA: You're probably right. It *is* my fault.

VOVA: It's not that you… There are ways to work on singing. To achieve an emotional response… from someone who is listening.

URZULA: But I didn't *know* you were listening.

VOVA: No. You didn't.

Long beat.

URZULA: You like my voice.

VOVA: As I said, it's fine.

Yes.

I like it.

Beat; she considers something.

URZULA: Do you like spying on me, listening to me?

VOVA: No. No I don't… That's not something I think about, whether I like something or not.

URZULA: You like my voice.

VOVA: I told you it was okay.

URZULA: How do you feel when you hear me laugh? Do you want to laugh with me? Or does my laugh annoy you.

VOVA: Both. Sometimes it has an irritating timbre.

URZULA: How do you feel when you hear me cry?
Are you sad that I am sad?

Beat.

VOVA: Yes. Or anyhow, I'm interested in why you're sad.
I can't tell all the time why you are.

URZULA: Do you think I'm a good person?

VOVA: Good and not good, these aren't considerations.

(Beat.)

But you have intentions to escape to the West, which is unlawful.
And so, bad.
No. I don't think you are a good person.

Beat.

URZULA: How do you feel when you hear me with a man?

Long beat.

URZULA: Do you like hearing that?

VOVA: No.

URZULA: Do you stop listening?

Long beat.

URZULA: *(She goes to him, sits near him.)* Let me see your fingers, the ones that got sucked.

Long beat.

VOVA: No.

URZULA: I can tell your fortune.

Babcia says the best way to tell a person's fortune is to smell their fingers just after they eat Qureshi.

(Beat.)

Do you want me to try?

VOVA: No.

URZULA: Why not? I can see who you will be one day and –

VOVA: *No.*

URZULA: *(Offers her hand.)* Then tell mine, my future.

VOVA: I can't, I have no sense of smell, and I don't believe this nonsense anyhow.

URZULA: Try.

She sits near him and gives him her hand. He looks at it… she touches his face, his mouth, his nose, dragging her fingertips over his face.

VOVA smells her fingers.

URZULA: Do you smell anything?

VOVA: *(Quietly.)* Yes.

URZULA: Describe it.

VOVA: I don't know how.

URZULA: Say something. What do you smell?

He thinks.

VOVA: Gasoline.
Fuel.
Fire.

(Beat; he sees something.)

You will die in an airplane crash…

(Beat.)

... holding that diary in your hands.

He starts to cry...

VOVA: I'm sorry... I'm so sorry... why did I...
I'm sorry I saw that...
I'm sorry I said that.

She takes his hand, where he had pricked his fingers. She kisses the tips of his fingers, and then smells them.

VOVA: Stop it. Stop doing this.

She kisses his fingers.

URZULA: Stop what?

VOVA: You're trying to seduce me.

She kisses his fingers, his hand...

URZULA: No.

VOVA: You're playing a game. You're trying to escape.

URZULA: No I'm not.

VOVA: This isn't who I am. This isn't me. This is wrong...

URZULA: No, it's not. You're good. You're a good man.

She kisses him, he kisses her back.

Transition:

Old YEVGENIA and Old NIKOLAI enter and look at each other with irritation. Through their irritation, they make each other young again. They undress each other, remove old hair, to reveal young hair.

YEVGENIA's hair is cut short, too short, and she wears a hospital gown. NIKOLAI wears his police uniform.

YEVGENIA exits, NIKOLAI goes to a bar in Moscow and drinks.

NIKOLAI stands at the bar. ISAAC enters.

ISAAC: Nikolai…

NIKOLAI: Babel!

ISAAC: I came as soon as I got your message.

NIKOLAI: Come. Stand here.
I've emptied this grimy tavern so we might talk alone.

ISAAC: Are you okay? You look terrible.

NIKOLAI: I haven't slept.

ISAAC: You should sleep.

NIKOLAI: This is serious.

ISAAC: What's going on?

NIKOLAI: Let's have a drink. Vodka. TWO VODKAS!

ISAAC: You're making me nervous.

NIKOLAI: Why, what do you have to be nervous about?

ISAAC: Nothing.

NIKOLAI: Everyone has something to be nervous about.

ISAAC: Okay.

NIKOLAI: You have plenty to be nervous about.

ISAAC: Tell me, please.

NIKOLAI: You should leave the country.

ISAAC: *What?*

NIKOLAI: France. Or something like France. *Paris.*

ISAAC: I can't do that.

NIKOLAI: What have you been up to?

ISAAC: In terms of…

NIKOLAI: Have you been doing shit?

ISAAC: I don't know what that means.

NIKOLAI: Good.

ISAAC: Good?

NIKOLAI: Things are bad. We might all need to leave the country.

ISAAC: Who's we?

NIKOLAI: Everyone.

ISAAC: Everyone in Russia?

NIKOLAI: Perhaps.

ISAAC: All Russians.

NIKOLAI: Perhaps.

ISAAC: All Russians need to leave Russia.

NIKOLAI: He wants everyone dead.

ISAAC: Who? *Stalin?*

NIKOLAI: Shhhh!!!! Just remember, remember what I told you. What did I tell you?

ISAAC: Never confess.

NIKOLAI: Even when they torture.

ISAAC: I'm going to be tortured?

NIKOLAI: Everyone is tortured! Nobody confesses as soon as they sit down.

ISAAC: So what if they torture it out of me?

NIKOLAI: NEVER CONFESS!

ISAAC: I know, but what if –

NIKOLAI: What if nothing! Never confess!
Now before it gets to that, get out of the country. Like, presently. Maybe Paris.

ISAAC: What about my work?

NIKOLAI: What about it?! Your work will kill you if you stay here. Leave. Meet me in Paris.

ISAAC: Meet *you?*

NIKOLAI: I also may be accused of some dreamt-up crime, and so I may be fleeing the country like you.

ISAAC: You might flee the country?

NIKOLAI: Now you understand! I'm telling you, nobody is safe.

ISAAC: But you'll bring Yevgenia, of course. You won't just leave her.

NIKOLAI: No, Yevgenia will not be coming.

ISAAC: You can't leave her!

NIKOLAI: Arrangements have been made. She is being protected.

ISAAC: Protected how?

NIKOLAI: I had her committed to the state asylum for the insane.

ISAAC: *WHAT?*

NIKOLAI: Quiet! Will you shut your mouth!? If I am seen speaking to you like this? Having a vodka with you like this? No! We will both be arrested. And then tortured and put to death. They wouldn't even ask us questions first. *So don't yell.*

ISAAC: *(Trying to be quiet.)* Yevgenia is not insane!

NIKOLAI: I am aware of this, but she knows too much. So she might as well be.

ISAAC: What does that *mean?*

89

NIKOLAI: It means, it's better than prison! What am I telling you!? Nobody is safe! Unless you are committed to the state asylum of the insane. Then they can't arrest you and take you in and torture you until you confess. And so Yevgenia is safe.

ISAAC: She's safe... So when does she get out?

NIKOLAI: Out of what?

ISAAC: *(Trying to be quiet, but can't contain himself.) I'm talking about the asylum, when does she get out of the asylum!*

NIKOLAI: You can't "get out" of the asylum. The insane don't suddenly become uninsane.

ISAAC: *She's not insane!*

NIKOLAI: Why are you so upset about this? This doesn't concern you.

Awkward beat.

ISAAC: Nikolai... *Your* wife should not be in an asylum.

NIKOLAI: I know that, you know that, but according to the state... Yevgenia is insane, and so... she will be insane forever and... That's the way it is.
She'll simply be there now. From now on.
It's better than prison.

ISAAC: I don't know if it is!

NIKOLAI: It is.

ISAAC: Which asylum is she in?

NIKOLAI: Moscow First Dominion. Best there is.

ISAAC: We are talking about your wife! Your *wife*, Nikolai!

NIKOLAI: *(Snide.)* She was less than that, ultimately.

ISAAC: What does that mean?

NIKOLAI: She was having an affair!

Beat.

ISAAC: Really? That doesn't sound like her.

(Beat.) How would you suspect something like that.

NIKOLAI: A husband's intuition.

ISAAC: Yeah, but I mean... You think she was having an affair?

NIKOLAI: Yes.

ISAAC: But with whom?

NIKOLAI: I *must* know the bastard. I must know *of* him at least. I don't imagine I'll ever find out. What idiot would ever confess to something like that. Sleeping with *my* wife!?

ISAAC: Nobody would ever confess.

NIKOLAI: As well they shouldn't.

They both finish their drinks.

NIKOLAI: Listen to me: Go to your study or office or whatever squallorous den it is where you write... and collect your works! Gather it all and take it with you!

ISAAC: Gather my works?

NIKOLAI: Put it in a box! Otherwise it will be found and dealt with. Do you want to be dealt with!? Or do you want to go to Paris?

(Beat.)

What if you and I, Isaac, what if you and I went to Paris.

ISAAC: You have to get Yevgenia!

NIKOLAI: Hypothetical notion! That say, for example, you and I left, the two of us, and went to Paris...

(He tries to imagine, but it's hard.)

What would life... what would that look like?

ISAAC: *(Bitterly, with anger about YEVGENIA.)* We would be foreigners. We would have thick accents. No one would read my work, nobody would salute or respect you… There are no rules in Paris and so… there is nothing for a Russian man there.

NIKOLAI: And here there is?

NIKOLAI slams his vodka.

I need to go.

ISAAC: Nikolai.

NIKOLAI suddenly, and not gently, holds ISAAC's face in one hand and looks deep into his eyes.

The way he's grabbed him could mean he's either going to kill him or kiss him.

NIKOLAI kisses him. Once on each cheek.

NIKOLAI: You are my friend and I love you.

NIKOLAI abruptly leaves. ISAAC suddenly sees YEVGENIA sitting in the corner. He is no longer in a bar, but rather, in an asylum for the mentally insane in Moscow in 1940.

YEVGENIA sits silently, staring into space. Her head is shaved. A sickening glow of institutional light fills the space. Echoes are heard, of an asylum.

ISAAC enters behind her and stares at her for a long moment.

ISAAC: Yevgenia. Yevgenia, what happened to your hair?

She turns to him slowly, sees him, takes him in, and then almost as if in slow motion, turns away from him, and tries to hide her head with her gown, ashamed.

It's okay, it's okay, it's okay, it's okay, it's okay...

(Beat.)

I know a doctor. I bribed him. That is how I am here, I am not allowed to visit you like this. I am sorry to surprise you, to come calling without notice, I know how you like fair warning, how you appreciate rules of society or wherever. But what else could I do? Yevgenia...

YEVGENIA: Why do you have a suitcase?

ISAAC: This is my work. Everything I could pack in. Everything I have written in the past few years... I need to take it with me everywhere I go because...

(Beat; he considers his work, then YEVGENIA.)

This is nothing.

(Beat.)

What is there for you to eat?

YEVGNIA: Cabbage. And cabbage soup.

ISAAC: To drink?

YEVGENIA: Water.

ISAAC: No tea?

YEVGENIA: No tea.

ISAAC: How could there not be tea?

YEVGENIA: No tea.

ISAAC: Where do you sleep?

YEVGENIA: A cot.

ISAAC: Is it comfortable?

YEVGENIA: No.

ISAAC: Are there activities for you to do during the day?

YEVGENIA: You must have paid the man a good sum to stand here now.

ISAAC: I did.

YEVGENIA: What did you ask?
　　If there are activities for me to do during the day?
　　I bite my fingernails.
　　And I sit alone and wonder how long before I start to lose my mind.

ISAAC: This place is a misery.
　　Yevgenia!

A loud slam echoes through the place from far away. It sounds like a gate crashing shut, but it could be almost anything. It startles ISAAC.

ISAAC: What can I do?

YEVGENIA finally turns again and looks at him. They look into each other's eyes from a distance.

YEVGENIA: Give me something to read…?

ISAAC: Something to read…? Of course, but I didn't bring any…

She gestures to his suitcase. ISAAC didn't realize she meant his work. That she did moves him immeasurably.

ISAAC: You mean… *my* work…?

He excitedly opens up his suitcase on the floor. It is indeed packed to the hilt with papers, journals, books, etc.

ISAAC: Of course! Of course, let me see... I could give you... *this!*

(He pulls out a stack of papers.)

These are stories I wrote about my hometown of Odessa! The gangsters and street crime there that...

(Changes his mind.)

No. Too gloomy. Not... *Inspiring* enough. Let me see...

(Looks through suitcase.)

Here! This is a novel I wrote about...

(Changes his mind.)

No, not this.

(Looks.)

THIS! This is the screenplay I wrote that you once recited about Daria and the ducks... and... oh.

YEVGENIA: Yes.

ISAAC: ... Daria is killed.

YEVGENIA: Yes.

ISAAC: You never liked that she was killed.

YEVGENIA: No.

ISAAC: *(Goes back to looking.)* Okay! Let's find something else! Something inspiring and humorous and lovely and... DAMNIT everything I have is about DEATH!
Why didn't I write anything about... how some magical, beautiful woman could walk through walls...

YEVGENIA: *(Trying to imagine, too.)* Walls, prison walls, like soft cheese.

ISAAC: Soft cheese, yes... and she could fly and she could walk on water...

YEVGENIA: That would be a perfect story. Too perfect. Too much.

(Beat.) Anything, dear Isaac... anything to read is fine.

ISAAC looks through his suitcase and then finally finds his journal.

ISAAC: Then take this.

This was my first journal. The diary I kept in Poland – when I met Nikolai.

This is why I am who I am.

He hands it to her, she takes it.

YEVGENIA: I am pregnant, Isaac.

Beat.

ISAAC: You are pregnant.

YEVGENIA: Yes.

ISAAC: Then we must devise a plan so that you might escape. Listen to me, Yevgenia, I will help you. We can't waste time. NOW. *NOW.* I can bribe the doctor.

YEVGENIA: You had to pay him simply to step foot inside of here. He will never risk his life to help an inmate escape.

ISAAC: I could set a fire in here right now. They would have to evacuate the entire building. And then we could run away into the night, and leave Russia and move to Paris and I will write and you can sing and act and we can be liberated Russian nationals and tell the world of the ills of this miserable Stalin rule.

YEVGENIA: Or we'd burn to death.

ISAAC: Or we could run off to Turkey and become Muslim.

YEVGENIA: Isaac...

ISAAC: We will get you out of here.

YEVGENIA: There is no way out.

ISAAC: You are pregnant…

YEVGENIA: Yes…

ISAAC: If you complain of pain in your womb, they will take you to another hospital.

YEVGENIA: I will be restrained.

ISAAC: But if we plan on when this might be, I can be there too, and I can cause a diversion, and I can unlock your restraints…

YEVGENIA: How.

ISAAC: I know a man. A locksmith. In fact, he *owes me*. He will be there to meet you at the specified time. He will unlock you and you can disappear into the night. Walk due west out of Moscow into the woods where I will be waiting with clothes, food, money and we can wend our way out of this endless land. And you will give birth to a… to a…

YEVGENIA: A girl, a daughter…

ISAAC: A daughter! And we will raise her as a true citizen of the world! Even further away… we can go to Northern Europe! Scandinavia! Some place cool and blue with ice floes and fjords.

YEVGENIA: Salted fish.

ISAAC: And tea.

YEVGENIA: And tea!

ISAAC: We will teach her the Russian preparation of tea, exiles who keep the best parts of their country, like how we will be drinking tea the proper way, hot, hot hot, until it sweats out of your stomach, until beads of tea appear on your belly, the hot way.

YEVGENIA: Condensation!

ISAAC: Our child will smile at people because she will never know the cruel gaze of communism. She will only know fjords and fish and tea.

YEVGENIA: And words. She will know words.

The *weight* of them… What is true and what is not true. She will speak to it, she will testify.

ISAAC: She will be an exiled Russian intellectual of the highest rank!

YEVGENIA: We will be so proud of her.

(Beat; quietly.)

… Fjords and fish and tea.

They hold each other for a moment, lost in a dream.

YEVGENIA: But how will I find you in the woods?

ISAAC: What?

YEVGENIA: After I fake illness, after I am brought, in restraints, to the maternity ward, after your locksmith friend loosens my chains, and I escape into the night, walking due west out of Moscow into the woods… how will I find you in the woods? Isaac, the woods spill out in every direction, and they are cold and damp and wild. You will be somewhere in the woods, how could I find you?

ISAAC: How will you find me.

YEVGENIA: How will I find you.

ISAAC: How will I find you…

YEVGENIA: How will you find me…?

Beat. They almost wake from their dream, and fall back into despair, until…

ISAAC: I will play a cello.

YEVGENIA: A cello!

ISAAC: I will play a cello in the woods. Stand in the woods, Yevgenia, and listen for the low thrum of a cello...

The sound of a cello playing, lonesome, far away is heard. They both hear it.

YEVGENIA: Where will you get a cello?

ISAAC: I know a cello-maker. He owes me. Can you hear it?

YEVGENIA: I hear it.

ISAAC: Listen for me in the woods, woman.
I will play for you until you are there, and you come to me, and we are together.

Bureau 42.

NIKOLAI, clad in a bathrobe, looking more past his prime, is asleep at his desk. He is having a nightmare… a mixture of moans, cries, snores… and then he is quiet.

VOVA enters from the elevator. He carries himself with confidence, swagger, he has a briefcase.

He sees NIKOLAI sleeping and puts the briefcase on the desk. VOVA rings his bell. But NIKOLAI doesn't awaken.

VOVA: Yezhov, N. N stands for Nikolai.
Born Petersburg, One May, 1895.

(Reading file.)

You served in the Russian Imperial Army, the Red Cavalry and thereafter Chief Commander of the NKVD.
You used to stand by Stalin's side. His right hand man!

(Flips through file.)

And then some details that seem decidedly false:
You were…
Executed for treason.
Buried in a mass grave.

(Surprised.)

And you were a dwarf!

NIKOLAI awakens suddenly.

NIKOLAI: *(Defensive; insecure.)* I'm not a dwarf!

VOVA: Your nickname: "The Poison Dwarf".

NIKOLAI: *(Frantically locates magic marker and wields it.)*
That's not my nickname! You don't call me dwarf!

VOVA: Also: "The Bloody Dwarf".

NIKOLAI: *(Holding up marker.)* I *erased* that! It is no longer official state knowledge!

VOVA: You no longer preside over official state knowledge.

VOVA hands NIKOLAI a form.

VOVA: Yezhov, N. You are hereby relieved of your duties as First Chief Directorate, Level Double 'A' and *Chairman* of Bureau 42.

NIKOLAI reads the form. He is stunned... disoriented...

NIKOLAI: *What is this...?* I was asleep... I'm still dreaming! Yes, that's it! I was having a nightmare ...

(Re-reads the form.) How...? Who...?

VOVA: *I* have been promoted to your position!

NIKOLAI: *YOU?!*

VOVA: I have been deemed an appropriate replacement! My file clearly indicates I am a superlative agent for the KGB. My record: impeccable. Never insubordinate. Expert in judo and all martial arts. Fluent in German, English and Chinese! My record states, even: I am a Good Man.

NIKOLAI: Good and Not Good, these are not –

VOVA: – Considerations! Yes. They are. These are now considerations. Changes abound. Modernity! The world has changed, Yezhov Comrade, and you are of a *different time.* And so, at long last, after a... confusing and misshapen career... you will finally retire from this business. Perhaps you might retreat to some coastal town... I hear Sochi is nice.

NIKOLAI: How dare you! Descending into *my* Bureau and tell me this...

VOVA: *(Points to form.)* Acknowledge the affidavit, please. It has been signed, stamped and confirmed by ranking members of the Kremlin!

NIKOLAI: THIS IS NOT OFFICIAL! You cannot simply tell me something and then expect to be… to be…

VOVA: … true?

NIKOLAI: You… You are a sub-standard, low-level… *thug.* You don't have the authority…

I am I am IN CHARGE HERE!

VOVA: *(Sharply; accusing.)* In 1940 you were designated an *unperson.*

But you did not accept this.

And so, in a flagrant violation of Soviet bylaws, you resurrected your existence.

And so you are insubordinate.

(Beat.)

Being alive when you are dead: This is against the law.

NIKOLAI: Don't tell me what is the law.

Don't tell me who is alive and who is dead.

You don't know your own life.

(Beat.)

And this is MY Bureau! No one else knows where to find things, I've spent *years* organizing every file!

VOVA: The information in this dank cell will be compressed and shrunken into microbytes of easily accessed data.

(Takes out a floppy disk, circa 1989.)

Behold Yezhov, the floppy disk! The most powerful tool in all of communism…

In the New Soviet Union, computers will be the key to *everything.*

He hands the disk to NIKOLAI who holds it as if he's never seen anything like it – with disgust and curiosity.

NIKOLAI wanders away from his desk in a daze. VOVA takes his place behind the desk.

NIKOLAI: Wait… WAIT…! What of my grand-daughter! You were to contain her! *That* is your current assigned mission! Where is she?

VOVA: Your grand-daughter… Urzula… I contained her.
She tried to escape and I prevented her from doing so. Better: I convinced her of acceptable alternatives to escape…

NIKOLAI: That was not your assignment! Insubordinate!

VOVA: I appealed to her deeper self. Her Russian roots. I implored her: Understand the blood in your veins.
And she did.
We fell in love.
She carries my child.

NIKOLAI: Ohhhh… I see… I see the games you play. Truth-Lies! Lies-Truth!
You learned from me these little games!

VOVA: No games. I eat dinner with her every night. We eat soup. Prepared by her grand-mother. *Yevgenia.*

NIKOLAI: That's a lie!

VOVA: No lie.

NIKOLAI: Yevgenia is dead! She died in the asylum!

VOVA: She is very much alive.

NIKOLAI: No! She died giving birth to a child!
And the child was whisked away — with millions of others — in the chaos of war.
This is why we built our wall in Berlin: To hold the earth steady… *so we could find the people who were lost to us.*
So I could find my daughter…

(Beat.)

So I could find my grand-daughter…

VOVA: Urzula is not your grand-daughter… She is no blood of yours.

She is the offspring of Isaac Babel, the Jewish writer.

NIKOLAI: No no no…

(He shuts his eyes tight; then recovers.)

So I will tell you a story! Everything you've said is a lie. This affidavit is a lie. Your stupid, pinchy face is a lie. Yevgenia is dead, Urzula is my blood, and by tomorrow morning you will be in Siberia, cleaning latrines with frozen washrags and spit.

VOVA: Urzula and I, and our child… AND Yevgenia… will repair to Leningrad. My birthplace, where my Mother lives, and we will raise our child together, and he will be a true citizen of the Soviet Union, a boy who will understand in his bones the virtues of Communism, the glory of Russia, the pride of Leningrad.

And he will be a champion at judo.

Like his father.

NIKOLAI: Ah… wait… ha ha… yes, I remember now! My dream! My hideous, awful nightmare…

It was about Gorbachev! That rascal! And his childish progressive notions of *Glasnost! Openness!* Do you know what results from "openness"? *Escape!* And in my dream, my nightmare, that Gorbachev, he was wearing the cowboy hat! And he was singing the rock-n-roll! And he tore down our wall. Our beautiful Berlin Wall, keeping us secure and safe from the lies of the West!

A rumbling is heard…

Do you hear it? Do you hear the rumbling of Glasnost… the clawing of demented youth, digging their way to the West!?

VOVA: You may leave now.

NIKOLAI: The Berlin Wall is Falling!

Listen for it! Go back to East Germany and see!

VOVA: This is nonsense what you are saying! Get out!

NIKOLAI: And what of *Urzula?*

Is she a young lady who waits for her Stasi Man?
Or is she already scampering West?
To Freedom... To Freedom! Ha!
To FREEDOM!

The rumbling increases... NIKOLAI shuffles away...

A wall of Bureau 42 suddenly crumbles into a rubble of stones...

A very pregnant URZULA, with a bag, and a coat, steps over the rubble... and into freedom.

VOVA watches in horror as she walks, holding her belly...

The distant rumble of rock and roll... builds...

Blackout and then music:

Loud, Anarchic, Rock-n-Roll... Free.

End of Act II.

Act III

YEVGENIA stands or sits looking out a window at the street sky outside.
She munches absently on sunflower seeds, or something like that.

She watches birds fly. She watches people on the street below.

YEVGENIA: Once upon a time…

There was a woman who could walk through walls.

(Beat.)

For her, walls were nothing except soft cheese.

No stone, rock, concrete or steel could hold her.

She would always find herself to the other side, where she
was free to seek out the life she desired.

When she comes to water: She walks on water.

When she comes to a mountain: She flies.

This woman is *free*.

(Beat.)

Ha.

Not really.

A violent knocking on the door until the door is forced open and VOVA
stumbles into the room, frantic.

VOVA: *Where is she?* Old Woman! Where is she?

YEVGENIA: Who?

VOVA: *Zula!* Where did she go?

YEVGENIA: Who can say?

VOVA: You can say! *You know… You know where she went.*

YEVGENIA: *(Sharply.)* You can't read minds, sonny! You'll
want to breathe in the asshole of a goat before you make
proclamations like that!

106

VOVA: Tell me she didn't leave Dresden!

YEVGENIA: Oh yeah, she did.

> *(Beat.)* Do we want soup?

VOVA: Where's that book? Where is that Babel book that she loves?

> *(Beat.)* She wouldn't leave you here! She wouldn't leave you all alone!

YEVGENIA: And who says Yevgenia doesn't have a say in the matter!? Me, who's been pushed about through the last ninety years like some wheelbarrow!
If I want to stay put for once, I'll stay put!

VOVA: She must have told you where she went!

YEVGENIA: *(As if she remembers something.)* Oh!

VOVA: What.

YEVGENIA: Come here…

VOVA: What is it?

YEVGENIA: I can tell you a secret, come…

VOVA: What, what is it…?

YEVGENIA: Listen…

VOVA: Yes?

YEVGENIA: *(Beat; then whispers.) There used to be more ducks in this lake.*

VOVA: What does that mean?

YEVGENIA: Means what it means! At one point, here, in this lake: Many ducks. Now? Less.

VOVA: You've lost your mind, old woman. *Where did she GO?!*

YEVGENIA: I heard they were all killed.

VOVA: Who? Who was killed?

YEVGENIA: What are we talking about? *Ducks!*

VOVA: Stop talking about ducks! I will find her!

YEVGENIA: Maybe, maybe not.

VOVA: I *will.* I will search every country in Europe to find a woman with a newborn child…

He sits at the table across from her. He now seems like a son, complaining to his mother.

VOVA: *(As if trying to explain.)* I will put this world back together to find her! I will put that wall back together, piece by piece!

(Beat; truly aggrieved.)

Why did she leave?
Why did she leave me?

In compassion, whether real or sarcastic, YEVGENIA takes his hand in hers.

YEVGENIA: Oh there, there…

VOVA: She carries my child. I am the father of that child.

YEVGENIA: *(Shrugs.)* You will survive this and other insults.

VOVA: *(Quietly.)* Don't mock me.

YEVGENIA: *(Studies his hand.)* Oh my. You have a bright young future in front of you do, don't you?
Oh My.
Look at all this.

VOVA: What?

YEVGENIA: You will be… very very very… *important.*

VOVA: What does that mean?
More of your witchcraft, Old Woman!?

She lets go of his hand dismissively.

YEVGENIA: Fine.

VOVA: No! What did you see?

YEVGENIA: Do you want soup?

He presses his hand in her hand.

VOVA: Do your witchcraft! Do it now! What do you see?

YEVGENIA looks more carefully at his hand.

YEVGENIA: Well…
One day, you'll be *President of Russia.*

He whips his hand away.

VOVA: *(With rage.) I said don't mock me!*

YEVGENIA: You'll do everything you ever wanted to do!
You'll tear the world apart to make another wall.
And after! After your world is back together in the bloated shape you desire, it will all come back for you.
Every misery, every push and shove, every bullet and belt, it will all come back. You will fight it. You will.
You will suck the blood of everyone around you to stay alive. You will suck my blood. You will drown sucking my blood. And I will eat you in a bowl of soup.

She goes back to her window and stares out.

She looks up at the birds.

She eats a sunflower seed.

YEVGENIA: Not that any of it matters. We're all going to drown in blood.
Look at that red sky.
There is nothing but war ahead.

SCENE 2. MORE LIES – 1940 – MOSCOW

An interrogation room.

ISAAC, badly beat up, sits in a chair, handcuffed to a desk. He may be unconscious, or he may be deep in thought.

His suitcase with pages of typed and written words is on a table near him.

NIKOLAI enters.

NIKOLAI: *(Reads from a paper.)* Babel, I. Writer.

You are accused of active participation in anti-Soviet Trotskyite organizations, of being a member of a terrorist conspiracy, and you are a spy for France.

(With distaste.)

A *French spy.*

You have written seditious, subversive, Anti-Soviet literature, and you have portrayed Joseph Stalin, on more than one occasion, as a duck.

How do you plead?

ISAAC: Nikolai…

NIKOLAI: How do you plead?

ISAAC: Nikolai, please…

NIKOLAI: You don't call me by this name. That is not my name. I am Chief Commander, you call me Chief Commander. Do you understand? How do you plead?

ISAAC: I deny everything. I didn't break a single law. I am not a spy. I am a loyal member of the Communist Party, I have never written ill of the Soviet Union or of Stalin, I have never portrayed him as a duck or as any bird or waterfowl. I was once a member of YugROSTA, stationed with the Red Cavalry in the Russo-Polish War in 1920.

I am a good man.

NIKOLAI: "Good" and "Not good" these are not the considerations.

ISAAC: I'm innocent!

NIKOLAI: You are NOT innocent!
> This: Your work! All of it: Subversive. Weird. Unorthodox. Trying too hard to be funny. Describing ugly things instead of beautiful things. Describing filth. Describing suffering. Describing Russia in such a way that does not inspire pride, but rather, a gloomy sense of doom.
> Do you deny you have written these pages?
>
> *(Beat.)* Do you deny you have written these pages?

ISAAC: Nikolai, those are...

NIKOLAI: You call me Chief Commander! And do you deny or do you not deny that you have written these words, all these words!?

ISAAC: I deny!

NIKOLAI: You're calling me a liar, then?

ISAAC: Not a liar, just mistaken. You have the wrong man.

NIKOLAI: I have the wrong man.

ISAAC: Yes.

NIKOLAI: So somebody else wrote these pages, these words.

ISAAC: Did you... Did you read the pages?

NIKOLAI: I need not wade through filth to know that it is filth.

ISAAC: *(With sudden unexpected rage.) Just because it is murky does not make it filth!*

> *(Beat; he speaks quickly, desperately.)*

> There is a story within that... case there... There are many stories, plays, poems, essays, notes, ideas, questions, exclamations, verses, doodles, sketchings, wonderments about the world... But there is one story in particular about a man – I want you to listen to this – a young soldier who has gotten lost in a strange land, separated from his troops,

and is all alone in some vast, terrifying countryside, trying to stay alive, trying to avoid enemy soldiers, wondering if he will ever find his comrades, or his way home, or see his friends again, or see his wife, whom he loves, even though he doesn't understand her and she doesn't understand him. *Because* he is lost, because he is more alone than he has ever been – more alone, in fact, than he ever thought anyone could ever be, he begins to discover truths about himself – for example that he doesn't understand his wife, and she doesn't understand him. It's about self-awareness...

NIKOLAI: Seditious. Topics like these: Self-awareness. No.

ISAAC: Let me finish.

He has been slowly walking east, in hopes of finding his division, or at the very least, his homeland.

NIKOLAI: Which homeland?

ISAAC: That's immaterial and not mentioned.

NIKOLAI: How could that be immaterial?

ISAAC: Immaterial for the purposes of the story.

NIKOLAI: The "purposes of the story" is to praise the Soviet Union! If not, you are engaging in some western mode of thinking that lauds "individuality" which always sounds fancy, but is in fact a wart upon the soul of mankind, and if you were loyal to Stalin you would understand this, but apparently you don't. And you have now admitted to writing these words, and so you have confessed –

ISAAC: I have not confessed! I never said anything about writing anything! I am just describing one of the pieces of writing within that case, which technically isn't a crime! Am I right?

NIKOLAI: You are mamby-pambying.

As ISAAC continues, NIKOLAI, in spite of himself, gets drawn into the story, and looks away, allowing himself to listen.

ISAAC: The lost soldier wanders east, and decides to stay the
night in a haystack. The night is a shivering cold: dry and
crisp, every breath blooms white.

He is awoken by a strange sound, and he walks around
the haystack to find an old man digging a hole. The man
is weeping, and before the soldier can hide, the old man
sees him, and just begins talking to him, as if they were old
friends, and not strangers, not enemies. The old man's son
has died of a fever, and he is now digging a grave in the
hard, frozen earth, and he is not making much progress.
The old man is weak, the body of his son, wrapped in a
cloth, is laid out to the side. The old man is overcome with
grief. He can't stop crying, and snot runs down his face...

NIKOLAI: Ugh...

ISAAC: So the soldier, not knowing what else to do, digs the
grave for the man. As he does, the old man explains that
he is alone now, he is the last of his family, and everyone
else's graves dot the premises. And when the grave is dug,
and the boy is lowered into it, the old man begins to sob,
uncontrollably, and the whole scene is actually rather
disgusting to the soldier, and not only that, but the old man
also has symptoms of a fever, and also an infection on his
hand that looks to be gangrenous.

So the soldier kills the old man with the shovel. In a
supreme act of pity. Of love, even. In a supreme act of
kindness, in a supreme act of self-interest. He buries the
man – the now peaceful man – with his son. He goes
to their distant hovel, eats their remaining stew, warms
himself by the fire, and realizes he does not love his wife.
And that if he never returned home, perhaps it wouldn't be
shameful or wrong. He longs for a place he has never seen,
a metropolis somewhere, where strangers commingle,
where men are kind, where there is no pity to be found
and nights are warm and cigarettes are cheap. A place
where men can love each other.

(Beat.)

Is there such a place? Where men can love one another?

(Beat.)

Maybe. The soldier wonders. Maybe.

A long beat.

NIKOLAI: *(So quiet he can barely be heard.)* What are you saying then?

ISAAC: What?

NIKOLAI: What are you SAYING THEN? I want to love men all of a sudden!?

ISAAC: The story isn't about you and even if it –

NIKOLAI: THAT STORY IS ALL ABOUT ME!
I know how you work. Never telling a story just the way it is! Always getting fancy!
I killed an old man because it *pleased me.* I didn't think about it before, I didn't think about it afterwards, I wasn't lost from my troop. And none of the other lying shit lies you've just said.

(Tries to regain his composure, reads.)

Babel, Isaac. Writer.
You are accused of active participation in anti-Soviet Trotskyite organizations, of being a member of a terrorist conspiracy, and...

(Breaks.)

You think I'm some faggot!? *Why?* Because my whore of a wife can't keep her legs shut for the entirety of Moscow!? Or is it something else. What did she tell you? What did she tell you about me?

ISAAC: Nothing.

NIKOLAI: What gives you the right to know her better than me? What gives her the right to whisper my secrets to any famous writer who comes to the door with cake?

I'm a man!

I am my own man!

I have a wife and a good job!

I fought in wars!

I am the Chief Commander of the NKVD, my parents would be so proud!

ISAAC: Yes… yes…

NIKOLAI: Why are things always symbols to you? Truth is lie, lie is truth. *Metaphor.* Do you want to see something that is not a metaphor?

NIKOLAI opens up a steel-shaft door in the wall, like a trash chute. It glows orange from within.

NIKOLAI: The furnace is not a metaphor.

Do you know what goes into the furnace and is burned and disappears forever?

Subversive and seditious writing.

He takes a ream of paper from the case.

ISAAC: Nikolai, no… no… please…

NIKOLAI dumps it down into the furnace.

ISAAC: THAT'S MY ONLY COPY! I DON'T HAVE ANYMORE, IT'S MY WORK YOU'RE BURNING! THAT'S MINE!

NIKOLAI takes more reams and dumps them into the flames.

ISAAC: WHY ARE YOU DOING THIS!? IT'S JUST STORIES! IT'S MY WORK! GOD DAMNIT, NIKOLAI?!

NIKOLAI: So you confess! You confess these are your writings!

ISAAC: YES! I CONFESS! EVERYTHING HERE IS MINE! Nobody else could have written any of it!

NIKOLAI: You confess!

ISAAC: YES! I confess!

NIKOLAI: Are you a terrorist, are you a French spy!?

ISAAC: NO!

NIKOLAI picks up more of the papers and stuffs them into the furnace.

ISAAC: YES! Okay, just stop! I'm a terrorist! I'm a member of an Anti-Soviet Trotskyite organization! I spy for the fucking French! Just stop burning my work!

NIKOLAI: You confess. You confess to all these crimes.

ISAAC: Just stop burning my work. My only copies...

A long beat. A terrible silence. Finally...

NIKOLAI: Did you engage in an extra-marital affair with Yevgenia Solomonovna?

Beat. They stare at each other.

ISAAC: The answer to such a question is so obvious that to even speak the words would make fools of us both.

NIKOLAI simply gathers the rest of the writing, and the case they were in and stuffs it all down the furnace.

ISAAC stares, can't even shout anymore, is emptied.

NIKOLAI: *Babel, I. Writer.* You are found guilty of terrorism, espionage, treason and writing subversive texts.

NIKOLAI turns to leave.

ISAAC: Nikolai, wait, please, wait, listen, you just have to let me...

(He begins to sob in panic.)

You have to let me finish!

You have to let me finish my work!

NIKOLAI, turns to ISAAC, takes out a gun and shoots him in the head.

He stares at ISAAC for a long moment, puts his gun away. He walks slowly to the door. For a moment he stops. He simply stands. He can't move. Then he opens the door and exits.

SCENE 3. SILENCE – 2010 – MOSCOW

The same interrogation room.

MARIYA sits at a desk. She looks fine—not beat up, not too stressed, as if the interrogation hasn't quite begun yet. There is a box on a table to the side.

VOVA enters.

MARIYA reacts the way someone might react if suddenly, instead of some police officer, the President of Russia suddenly walked into the room.

She recoils and stares at him...

MARIYA: *(Stammering.)* What are you...
    Why are you...
    What do you...

VOVA: Shhhh shh shhh shhhh...

MARIYA: Mr. President, I...

VOVA: Shhhh......

> *He goes to the box. From within methodically takes out items, and places them on the table*

Bus pass. Lip balm. Cash. A .38 caliber pistol. A pair of handcuffs. With keys. A nail file. A laptop computer that has curiously, suspiciously even, been erased of any information. Cleaned out.
And a condom.
But no photo ID.
Paints quite a picture, whomever you are.

(Whispers in mock secrecy.)

I know who you are.

Finally from inside the box, he takes out Babel's journal.

VOVA: One last thing. This. A very, very old book.
    A unique book.
    How do you have it?

(Beat.)

Ah.

Silence.

I respect silence.

(Beat.)

This is an old room.

In the 1930s and in the 1940s... this was called a *confessional booth.*

As a joke.

But this is no longer an operational precinct.

People are no longer brought here for questioning. You are special.

You *are* special, aren't you?

(Beat.) Do you know what this book is?

MARIYA: No.

VOVA: And isn't it interesting!

First, there was: *Silence.*

A wall of silence offered by: *You.*

Now, there is: "No".

Isn't that interesting. I didn't even have to use techniques.

Do you know what I mean by the word "techniques"? It's a fancy word for something not so fancy. "Techniques."

Do you know what this term means?

MARIYA: Yes.

VOVA: Ah! And now: "Yes." Again, without techniques.

Yes.

Do you know what techniques have taught us? They have taught us one absolute truth. Would you like to know what it is, this absolute truth? *Everyone. Speaks.*

(Beat.)

Do you think you are going to die today? Answer yes or no.

MARIYA: No.

VOVA: No. Good. I agree with you. Nobody wants anyone to die.

(Beat.) Of course, some people have, of course, died.

In this room, so many people:

Back then things were much much much different than they are today.

Back then, the head of the NKVD, a monster named Nikolai Yezhov, proclaimed that "It would be better that ten innocent men die than one traitor go free."

This is hardly a sustainable justice. Yes?

MARIYA: Yes.

VOVA: *Yes!* Yes yes yes yes.

Of course, many have died.

You would agree?

MARIYA: Yes.

VOVA: *Yes.*

Your friend, Yuri Egorov, who like you, was a reporter, your friend, tragically, was a victim of street crime. Yes?

(Beat.)

Mariya, yes?

MARIYA : Yes.

VOVA: Yes.

MARIYA: No.

VOVA: No?

MARIYA: *(Whispers,)* No.

VOVA: But this is a fact. It was officially designated as so. Go to the public records, find his death certificate. Yuri Egorov was robbed at gunpoint and then shot and killed. This is a fact.

You appreciate facts, don't you? As a journalist?

MARIYA: He was not a victim of street crime.

VOVA: Well.

Perhaps you prefer conjecture. Speculation. *Lies.*

MARIYA: No, I don't prefer lies, I prefer to not lie, I prefer to not build a world of lies to hide behind. Like a frightened little boy.

VOVA: Is that comment directed at me?

(Beat.)

Do I look frightened to you? Tell the truth.

MARIYA: A man who arrests journalists, kills journalists... a man who desires only for journalists to sing his praises... that looks like a frightened man to me.

VOVA: Perhaps we could play a game: "Who becomes more frightened". The winner gets to be... *not frightened.*

She stares at him for a moment, gauging how frightening this is...

MARIYA: Okay.

VOVA: Why do you *think* you are here?

MARIYA: I was in Smolensk the night of the Polish airline crash.

VOVA: You are a reporter for the Gazeta! You were on assignment to cover a diplomatic event, this is no crime. Why would this warrant your arrest?

She is silent.

Of course, tragedies such as the Smolensk crash –political ones, with global implications – these always suffer the insult of *conspiracy theory.*
Malevolent forces are shooting airplanes down from the skies!
Media outlets indulging in this behavior should be punished, wouldn't you agree?

(Beat.)

Or is this something you are engaged in. Are you writing lies you intend to publish? About that morning in Smolensk.

MARIYA: No.

VOVA: That's a lie.

MARIYA: It's not.

VOVA: In the seven months since the Smolensk crash, you have quit your job at the Gazeta, moved to Poland, and commenced erratic behavior including an attempt at changing your name, an attempt at acquiring a fake passport, the purchase of a firearm, and a meeting with a Polish filmmaker who has made it his purpose in life to spread lies about that crash. So I don't believe you when you tell me you're not one of the liars out there aiming to disgrace the memories of people far better than yourself.

(Beat.) People who lie are scum.

(Beat.) How are we doing with our game? I can assure you I am far from being frightened, so I'm confident I can win. Are you confident you can win?

She just stares at him, which suggests that she might be hanging in there. She does not betray fear.

He picks up Babel's diary.

VOVA: Where did you get this book?

MARIYA: A woman gave it to me.

VOVAL: A woman?

MARIYA: Yes.

VOVA: That's a lie.

MARIYA: It's not a lie.

VOVA: This book was given to you by a car rental clerk in Smolensk. Name of Feliks. He was brought in for questioning shortly after the crash. There was nothing suspicious about his whereabouts or behavior so he was let go. He seemed... insignificant.

We had "bigger fish to fry".

You, for example. A woman reporter who had gone missing. Your supervisors at the Gazeta had no idea where you were.

So we tapped your office phone.

And who should call one day, months after the crash?

An insignificant car rental clerk named Feliks.

So he was taken back into custody.

And after a lengthy conversation with him in a room not unlike this one, he confessed to so much... including that he gave you this book.

(Beat.) If it is of any comfort to you... "techniques" were necessary to acquire this information.

She takes this in, quietly, momentarily mourns FELIKS.

VOVA: This book is the original diary of the Russian writer Isaac Babel. He was a homosexual and one of the great liars of his age. He betrayed his fellow writers and was a spy for the French government.

VOVA inspects a file.

MARIYA: Have you read it?

VOVA: What?

MARIYA: The diary, have you read it?

VOVA: I've perused it. He was a bad writer. It's bad writing. You read it?

MARIYA: I read it.

VOVA: And?

Beat.

MARIYA: It made me want to write… about different things.

VOVA is irritated by this diversion, and shrugs it off and inspects a file.

VOVA: According to the car rental clerk, he purchased Babel's diary from a bookseller in Warsaw and never knew of its import. He said you saw it on his desk and asked to purchase it and he sold it to you.
Is that true?

MARIYA: Yes.

VOVA: *(Again refers to file.)* But then, at the time, this confession did not *seem* true! And so more techniques were used.
"Feliks" then confessed that he gave it to you in exchange for sexual favors. Intercourse.
The men questioning him, they believed this.

MARIYA: It's true. Yes.

VOVA: That's true?

MARIYA: Yes.

VOVA: Because that seems like a lie to me.

MARIYA: It's not.

VOVA: You fucked a man for a book?

MARIYA: I like to read.

VOVA: Ha. You have mettle, Mariya Tokareva. But you are a bad liar. Why don't you ask me a question. You must have questions for me.

MARIYA: No.

VOVA: No questions? A journalist gets to have a private audience with *Me*… and she has no questions?
Come now, Mariya… you strike me as a curious girl.

MARIYA: Was the Smolensk crash an assassination?

VOVA: What a question.

MARIYA: That's all it is.

VOVA: It was a terrible tragedy. An unfortunate accident that took place in the dark of dawn, in a thick fog, over the Katyn Forest.

(Beat.)

Do you know President Kaczynski was coming to Smolensk to honor the Katyn Massacre?

MARIYA: Yes, I knew that. That's why I was there. That's why Yuri was there.

VOVA: The Katyn Massacre. 20,000 Poles were murdered in that forest by the Nazis in 1940.

MARIYA: It wasn't the Nazis.

VOVA: According to some people. Everyone has competing narratives, isn't it so?

MARIYA: It's not so.

VOVA: Perhaps you like Nazis.

MARIYA: I don't like Nazis, but they didn't... they didn't do that. It wasn't the Nazis. It was Russia. Gorbachev admitted as much after the Berlin Wall fell.
It was the NKVD who killed those Poles. Not the Nazis.

VOVA: This is what happens when misinformation is pressed hard enough. Blame gets passed from one people to another. It is our burden now.

(Beat.)

The plane crashed at the very site of that mass grave. Where they had been executed seventy years earlier...

MARIYA: ... On the exact anniversary of the massacre.

VOVA: *(Smiles.)* The world is mysterious.

(Beat.) Now, this diary. Isaac Babel's diary is a lost Russian artifact designated by the Kremlin as a Top Level Interest. We have a list of things that belong to us, things that have been lost to time.

We want them back.

(Beat.)

I put this book on the list myself. I have been looking for it for twenty-one years. That's why I'm here right now. Where did you get this book, Mariya? I don't believe Feliks, I think he was a liar.

MARIYA stares at him for a moment, and then begins...

MARIYA: We were in the press room at the airport.

I went outside. The plane was delayed anyhow, they said.

VOVA: Why did you go outside?

MARIYA: To smoke.

VOVA: There are no cigarettes in your bag.

MARIYA: I quit.

VOVA: Good for you, it's a filthy habit.

MARIYA: Outside, I saw the forest. And I was smoking...

And then the plane crashed.

(She is quiet.)

And then there is fire everywhere... Darkness and blazing light. And I don't know why, but I ran towards it, the crash. And then there was a woman sitting in front of me. She was still in her seat, her seat had been torn out. She was sitting there. A piece of metal in her neck.

And she was holding that book. And she was smiling. She held it out for me. "Take this, dear..." She said. And I did. And then she died.

VOVA: That's a lie.

MARIYA: It's not —

VOVA: That is a LIE. Stop talking. I know the woman who
    owned this book, and she was not on the Smolensk flight,
    that is a fact, and so I know you are lying to me.

MARIYA: Ninety-seven people died in that crash. Of those,
    twenty-one were women. I went to Poland, I talked to
    people, I studied state files. I narrowed my search until I
    found her. Her name was Izabella Gorniak.

VOVA: Whoever that is, she did not own this book, so again I
    want you to tell me *where did you get it?*

MARIYA: Izabella Gorniak was not her real name.
    The woman had changed her name.
    She used to be called Urzula Solomonovna.
    She was the grand-daughter of Isaac Babel.

    Long beat.

VOVA: That's not... How do you know that is true?

MARIYA: I spoke to her grandmother.

VOVA: *(Slams table; begins to get up.) No you didn't.* This is over. I
    am finished playing games!

MARIYA: Her name is Yevgenia.

    Beat.

VOVA: *(Quietly; frightened.) Yevgenia.*

MARIYA: She lives alone in an apartment in Warsaw. She is
    110 years old. But she's spry.

    (Beat.)

    She was heart-broken about her grand-daughter's death.
    I tried to give her the diary, but she insisted I keep it.
    We spoke for many hours. We held hands while we talked.
    She made me soup.

    Beat.

VOVA: *(Quietly; frightened.)* Were there leeches in the soup?

MARIYA: *Leeches?* No…

(Beat.)

She told me Urzula had escaped from East Germany after the wall fell, given birth to a boy, and then given the child up for adoption. She said the father of the boy had been a Stasi agent, who had threatened Urzula with arrest if she didn't sleep with him. Yevgenia said he was a clown, with many faces, faces he had cut off of people who wronged him. She said that clown …

(In this moment MARIYA realizes who the clown in.)

… She said he would be the most powerful man in the world one day… but that he would never know his own blood.

(Beat.)

What could she have meant by that, do you think?

VOVA gets up and walks away, shaken. Trying not to show it.

A long beat. VOVA suddenly turns back to her. He stands behind her, she can't see him.

MARIYA: Ah.

Silence.

I respect silence.

Tears are in his eyes. He stares at MARIYA, not knowing whether to believe her or not.

Everything becomes brighter… a pulse becomes louder and louder until… Blackout. Within the darkness is heard a cello…

Transition:

Within the darkness of a wooded area… The cello continues, more distant.

YEVGENIA, having escaped from the asylum, walks through the woods, very pregnant. She clutches Babel's diary.

She hears the cello, and is trying to follow it, but gets confused. She switches directions… the source of the cello is difficult to find.

FELIKS enters, wearing a winter coat and a backpack. He has old bruises all over his face.

YEVGENIA stands behind, or to the side of him. He pays her no attention.

YEVGENIA: Do you hear a cello?

I'm looking for a man playing a cello for me in the woods. Have you seen him?

He doesn't answer. He doesn't seem to notice her at all. Or he is willfully ignoring her.

YEVGENIA: *(The cello begins to fade.)* He's playing for me. He always said he would play for me.

(Beat.) You can't hear the music?

He doesn't look at her when he speaks.

FELIKS: It's the wind.

YEVGENIA: *(Listens.)* Yes, the wind…

(Beat; listens more.) But on top of the wind… a cello.

FELIKS: Nobody's playing a cello.

YEVGENIA: In the woods, he plays.

FELIKS: There are no woods! There is no cello, and nobody's playing it.

YEVGENIA looks at him curiously.

YEVGENIA: Boy… Look at me. You are a beautiful boy. You have my Isaac's eyes. Look at me.

FELIKS: No.

YEVGENIA: Please.

FELIKS: No.

Long beat. They stand there, separately.

FELIKS: There is no cello, and nobody's playing it.

This is a bus stop and there is a bus and it is coming and when it gets here, I'm going to get on it and go to sleep.

(Beat.) All I want to do is to fall asleep on a bus.

They stand in silence.

YEVGENIA: I don't like to sleep.

I'm always afraid if I sleep, I will forget everything.

(Beat.) Almost everything gets forgotten, and what little is remembered becomes The Truth. It cannot be trusted!

(Sighs, sad; listens.) All that can be trusted is the cello.
Played through the night, by the one you love who may already be dead
A song of impossibility.

(Beat.)

Only the cello is true.

The cello comes in again.

YEVGENIA and FELIKS both hear it.

He turns and looks at her, she looks at him, takes him in. It makes her so happy, but she tries not to show it too much.

YEVGENIA: Do you hear my Isaac playing?

FELIKS: Yes.

YEVGENIA: *Yes.*

(Beat.)

Where is it coming from?

They look around.

FELIKS: I don't know. *Somewhere.*

Then they both look in the same direction. They both take a small step in that direction to hear better.

YEVGENIA: It's coming from there.

FELIKS: Yeah.

She's starts to leave, but then turns to him. She smiles at him.

YEVGENIA: You remind me of someone I have known forever.

Then she's gone.

FELIKS watches her go then turns back and faces forward, looks for the bus.

A bus approaches… lights flicker…

MRS. PETROVNA folds from a large basket of laundry. Sheets, etc.

She is a sturdy woman in her sixties. Tough as nails. She wears an eyepatch.

FELIKS enters.

MRS PETROVNA: We're closed. Come back tomorrow.

FELIKS: Hello.

MRS PETROVNA: Hello, come back tomorrow.

FELIKS: I'm a friend of Mariya Tokareva.

Beat; she stares at him.

MRS PETROVNA: What friend?

FELIKS: My name is Feliks.

MRS PETROVNA: You're Feliks? The orphan with a truck.

FELIKS: Yes.

Beat.

MRS PETROVNA: She's dead.

FELIKS: *(Barely keeping it together.)* I know. I saw. I came up here to find her and then I read about it in the paper. "A victim of street crime."

FELIKS and MRS PETROVNA stare at each other, both deeply sad.

MRS PETROVNA: Street crime. These days, a big problem.

FELIKS starts to cry, hides his face so she can't see.

FELIKS: It's my fault! I told the police! I told them! I'm sorry…

MRS PETROVNA: *(Irritated.)* Shut up.

FELIKS: I'm sorry… it's my fault…

MRS PETROVNA: *(Sharply; angry.)* Quiet, okay? You want credit! No!

She's dead, street crime, whatever street crime.

(For a moment sad.) She was brave.

(Back to being angry; irritated.) You can be either brave or smart, but never both.
Mariya happened to be brave.
I'm neither. Cowardly, stupid and old. That is who I am.

Beat. She angrily folds laundry. He watches her.

MRS PETROVNA: Do you want to stand there or do you want to leave or do you want to be useful and fold?

He doesn't know what to do. He just stands there looking at her.

FELIKS: What happened to your eye?

She looks at him, and then back to her folding.

MRS PETROVNA: A dog bit my face.

FELIKS: What kind of dog?

MRS PETROVNA: What the hell does that matter? A dog!

FELIKS: Sorry, I'm not thinking right.

MRS PETROVNA: What kind of dog! Go away.

FELIKS: I'm sorry. They punched me so hard I can't see things. Sometimes. I've been seeing visions. I think I see people. Men with fists. Men in shadows. Broken trees and seats in the ground. A pregnant woman in the snow. Nothing makes sense.

(Beat.) I saw a plane crash.

She nods.

FELIKS: And I met a woman and she was about to die. And she called me "son" and now, because I'm stupid and lost and seeing things because of my busted eye, now I'm thinking, yeah, that's her, she's definitely my mother. That woman, by pure coincidence, is the mother I never met.

Why would I do that to myself?

MRS PETROVNA: That woman wasn't your mother!

Beat.

FELIKS: How do you know that?

MRS PETROVNA: I don't, I'm guessing! Just like you.

FELIKS: I'm sorry I came here… I have to go.

MRS PETROVNA: Boy… You have two hands? You can fold? Stay here. Fold. And you need a place to sleep, upstairs, there's a room.

Beat; he's almost embarrassed by her kindness.

FELIKS: I don't know how to fold laundry.

MRS PETROVNA: It's not rocket science.

FELIKS: You don't understand.

MRS PETROVNA: What don't I under/stand–

FELIKS: – I'm not gonna fold laundry! I'm not gonna stay upstairs! They killed Mariya, and they beat me senseless, and…

(Beat; with some anger, confusion.) Why are you trying to *help* me?

She shrugs.

MRS PETROVNA: Why not? Do unto others, and so forth.

FELIKS: People don't just help people for no reason.

MRS PETROVNA: Who says I got no reason? I need the help! The whole of Moscow drops their linens here, feels like to me.

FELIKS: The world is just fucked okay? And I'm not gonna find any comfort or safety or ANYTHING from you or some beat up old laundry.

MRS PETROVNA: *(Looks around; feigning insult.)* I mean… I try to keep the place up…

FELIKS: Sorry, I didn't mean…

MRS PETROVNA: You apologize too much. Quit that.
And anyhow, this place… It isn't a laundry, not now.

FELIKS: It's not?

MRS PETROVNA: No. This here… this is a *kitchen.*

FELIKS: A kitchen?

MRS PETROVNA: Yes, yes a kitchen… And these washers and dryers, humming about, they are pots on a stove, coming to a boil. And this basket of warm clothes is a fire in the hearth. Warming us.

FELIKS stares at the basket of clothes, then at her. He reaches his hands out, as if to warm them by a fire. He shuts his eyes. He's in a warm kitchen, and she's there too. He's going to be okay.

MRS PETROVNA: Maybe it's almost time for supper.

It's quiet. The wind moans. They fold laundry together.

End of play.

WWW.OBERONBOOKS.COM

CPSIA information can be obtained
at www.ICGtesting.com
Printed in the USA
LVHW020349131219
640281LV00015B/1552/P

9 781786 823762